My
Kindle Fire

Jim Cheshire

que®

800 East 96th Street
Indianapolis, Indiana 46240 USA

My Kindle Fire

Copyright © 2012 by Pearson Education, Inc.

ISBN-13: 978-0-7897-4922-2
ISBN-10: 0-7897-4922-X

Library of Congress Cataloging-in-Publication Data is on file.

Printed in the United States of America

Second Printing: March 2012

Trademarks

All terms mentioned in this book that are known to be trademarks or service marks have been appropriately capitalized. Que Publishing cannot attest to the accuracy of this information. Use of a term in this book should not be regarded as affecting the validity of any trademark or service mark.

Warning and Disclaimer

Every effort has been made to make this book as complete and as accurate as possible, but no warranty or fitness is implied. The information provided is on an "as is" basis. The author and the publisher shall have neither liability nor responsibility to any person or entity with respect to any loss or damages arising from the information contained in this book.

Bulk Sales

Que Publishing offers excellent discounts on this book when ordered in quantity for bulk purchases or special sales. For more information, please contact

U.S. Corporate and Government Sales

1-800-382-3419

corpsales@pearsontechgroup.com

For sales outside of the U.S., please contact

International Sales

international@pearson.com

EDITOR-IN-CHIEF
Greg Wiegand

ACQUISITIONS EDITOR
Loretta Yates

DEVELOPMENT EDITOR
Todd Brakke

MANAGING EDITOR
Sandra Schroeder

PROJECT EDITOR
Mandie Frank

COPY EDITOR
Charlotte Kughen

INDEXER
Erika Millen

PROOFREADER
Leslie Joseph

TECHNICAL EDITOR
Kathleen Anderson

PUBLISHING COORDINATOR
Cindy Teeters

DESIGNER
Anne Jones

COMPOSITOR
Bronkella Publishing

Contents at a Glance

Table of Contents

About the Author

Jim Cheshire is a technology expert with a passion for gadgets. He's written about a dozen books and many online articles on technology, and is the author of the best-selling Kindle guide, *Using Kindle*.

Jim has a unique way of explaining technical concepts without being technical, a talent that has helped make his books and websites a leading resource for people who want to learn about technology in a fun and exciting way.

You can contact Jim through his website at www.MyAmazonKindleFire.com.

Dedication

This book is dedicated to everyone who has experienced the thrill of discovering the magic of the Kindle Fire. The excitement of the Kindle Fire community is truly an inspiration to me.

I'd also like to dedicate this book to my wife, Becky, and to my kids. You've been immensely supportive during this project and I love you for that.

Acknowledgments

This book would not have been possible were it not for the small army of people at Que Publishing who work tirelessly to support me. I owe a great deal of gratitude to Loretta Yates who always makes me feel like I'm the only author she has to deal with. Thanks also go to Todd Brakke and Charlotte Kughen, both of whom did a great job of editing my work and offering creative ideas for additional content, and thanks to Kathleen Anderson for reviewing the technical content for accuracy. Thanks also go to Mandie Frank and others who worked so hard to turn the hundreds of screenshots into the high-quality work you now hold in your hands.

We Want to Hear from You!

As the reader of this book, *you* are our most important critic and commentator. We value your opinion and want to know what we're doing right, what we could do better, what areas you'd like to see us publish in, and any other words of wisdom you're willing to pass our way.

As an editor-in-chief for Que Publishing, I welcome your comments. You can email or write me directly to let me know what you did or didn't like about this book—as well as what we can do to make our books better.

Please note that I cannot help you with technical problems related to the topic of this book. We do have a User Services group, however, where I will forward specific technical questions related to the book.

When you write, please be sure to include this book's title and author as well as your name, email address, and phone number. I will carefully review your comments and share them with the author and editors who worked on the book.

Email: feedback@quepublishing.com

Mail: Greg Wiegand
Editor-in-Chief
Que Publishing
800 East 96th Street
Indianapolis, IN 46240 USA

Reader Services

Visit our website and register this book at quepublishing.com/register for convenient access to any updates, downloads, or errata that might be available for this book.

Introduction

Your Kindle Fire is an amazing device. When you first power it on, it's a bit impersonal, but after you've connected to the Internet and registered the Kindle Fire with your Amazon.com account, something magical happens. All of a sudden, it begins to fill with your books and your music, and it becomes uniquely yours.

The fun doesn't stop there. You can look at your pictures, watch videos, play games, browse the Web, and get apps that enhance the capabilities of your Kindle Fire. Oh, and let's not forget that it's a Kindle, so you can read books, magazines, and newspapers as well.

At its heart, the Kindle Fire is all about consuming content in the *cloud*, content that is stored at Amazon. You access that content over a Wi-Fi connection. You can download content to your device, at which point it becomes *device* content, but a copy remains in the cloud as well. Does that sound confusing? Don't worry. It won't be after you read this book.

A Kindle Fire Overview

There's a lot packed into your Kindle Fire. Other Kindles are designed to be e-readers and don't really do anything else particularly well. Your Kindle Fire, on the other hand, is not just an e-reader. It's also an entertainment device, a content-consumption device, and a handheld computer. In fact, you'll find that many of the things that you typically do on your computer are more conveniently done on your Kindle Fire.

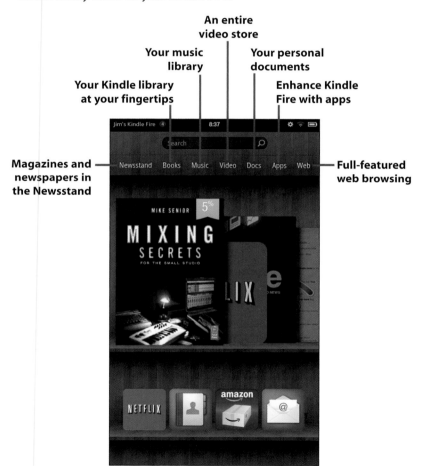

An entire video store

Your music library

Your personal documents

Your Kindle library at your fingertips

Enhance Kindle Fire with apps

Magazines and newspapers in the Newsstand

Full-featured web browsing

Here are just some of the things you can do with your Kindle Fire.

- Read newspapers and magazines in full-color.

- Read books from your Kindle library and from your local library as well.

- Listen to your music, discover new music, and buy music.

- Watch movies and TV shows, many of which are free to Amazon Prime members.

- Read personal documents in many formats, including Microsoft Word, PDF, and more.

- Enhance and add to the functionality of your Kindle Fire with apps from Amazon's app store.

- Browse the Web and even view Flash animations and video.

All of this functionality is provided in a nicely sized tablet that you can easily hold in one hand. Your Kindle Fire is, indeed, a great computer for sitting on the couch or in your favorite easy chair.

Why You'll Love *My Kindle Fire*

The Kindle Fire is a tablet computer for the rest of us. It's designed for people who aren't computer geeks and who just want to be entertained, read a good book, or have fun. *My Kindle Fire* was written with that same mindset. Of course, if you are a computer geek, this book can help you as well.

The book covers all of the capabilities of your Kindle Fire. I show you how to get the most out of each feature using a step-by-step approach, complete with figures that correspond to each step. You never have to wonder what or where to tap. Each task shows you how to interact with your Kindle Fire using simple symbols that illustrate what you should do.

This icon means that you should tap and hold an object on the screen.

 This icon means that you should drag an item on the screen.

 This icon indicates that you should pinch on the screen.

 This icon means that you should "reverse pinch."

 This icon indicates that you need to swipe on the screen.

Along the way, I add plenty of tips that help you better understand a feature or a task. I also warn you with It's Not All Good sidebars when you need to be careful with a particular task or when there are pitfalls that you need to know about. If you're the kind of person who likes to dig a little deeper, you'll enjoy the Go Further sidebars that provide a more in-depth look at particular topics.

Finally, for those of you with the paperback version of this book, you might notice that it isn't a big and bulky book. It's a handy size for taking with you when you go places with your Kindle Fire. That way, you can always find the steps necessary to do what you want to do. Of course, if you'd prefer not to carry the book with you, you can always purchase the Kindle Edition and read it on your Kindle Fire.

What You'll Find in the Book

Your Kindle Fire is full of surprises. The major functions are easy to discover, but some of the neater features are hidden away. As you read through this book, you'll find yourself saying, "Wow, I didn't know I could do that!" This book is designed to invoke just that kind of reaction.

Here are the things we'll cover in this book.

- Chapter 1, "Getting Started with the Kindle Fire", walks you through the initial setup of your device and how you can access some of the common settings. You'll also learn how to use touch to operate your Kindle Fire and how to use the onscreen keyboard.

- Chapter 2, "Amazon's Cloud Services", takes you on a tour of the online services that Amazon offers. Because these are the services that drive a lot of the Kindle Fire's functionality, you'll benefit from learning how they work and what they offer.

- Chapter 3, "Reading on the Kindle Fire", describes how you can get reading material for your Kindle Fire and how to take advantage of the Kindle Fire's powerful features for reading books, newspapers, magazines, and more.

- Chapter 4, "Using Amazon's Manage Your Kindle Page", shows you how to access the Manage Your Kindle page where you can look at your Kindle library, rename your Kindle Fire, manage your Kindle Fire and other Kindle devices, and much more.

- Chapter 5, "Managing Content with Calibre", introduces you to Calibre, a free application that makes managing your eBook library a breeze. Calibre allows you to manage third-party eBooks (ones you get from places other than Amazon) and even convert and transfer them to your Kindle Fire.

- Chapter 6, "Accessing and Listening to Music", shows you how you can use your Kindle Fire to play music in your music library (both music on your device and in the cloud) and how you can use Amazon's MP3 store to add to your music collection. You'll also learn about using playlists and other more advanced features.

- Chapter 7, "Watching Video", covers using your Kindle Fire to stream and download videos from Amazon's video store. You'll also learn how you can convert your own videos so that you can play them on your Kindle Fire.

- Chapter 8, "Installing and Using Apps", introduces you to the world of apps that dramatically increase the functionality of your Kindle Fire. You'll find out how to shop for apps, how to install apps, how to deal with apps that misbehave and cause problems, and you'll learn about some of the apps that you should definitely install on your Kindle Fire.

- Chapter 9, "Reading and Sending Email", will show you how to use your Kindle Fire to read and send email. You'll also learn about how to handle attachments in email and how you can add and manage contacts.

- Chapter 10, "Browsing the Web with Silk", walks you through using Silk, the web browser that comes with your Kindle Fire. You'll learn how to access websites, how to use bookmarks, how to use tabs, and how you can control Silk's behavior.

Let's Light This Fire

If you've already gone through the initial stages of setting up your Kindle Fire, you might be tempted to skip ahead to Chapter 2 at this point. I urge you not to. There are some hidden gems in Chapter 1 that you won't want to miss.

Now that the stage is set, let's light this fire. (Sorry. I couldn't resist.)

View all of your Amazon
content from the Carousel

Configure your
Kindle Fire

Add your favorite content
to the Favorites shelf.

In this chapter, you connect your Kindle Fire to your Wi-Fi network, register it with Amazon (if it's not already registered), and discover the basics of navigating and using your tablet. Topics include the following:

1

→ The Hardware
→ Initial Setup
→ Basic Usage of the Kindle Fire
→ The Home Screen
→ Notifications and Options
→ Settings
→ Searches
→ The Kindle Fire Keyboard

Getting Started with the Kindle Fire

The Kindle Fire is unassuming at first glance. However, after you power it on, you soon realize that it opens up a new world of entertainment and information. Couple it with Amazon's wide range of services, and the Kindle Fire becomes a truly extraordinary device. In fact, it's likely that in addition to being a great reading device, your Kindle Fire might replace your computer for many of the things you do on the Internet.

The Kindle Fire is not difficult to use. Many of its features are intuitive and you can easily discover many of the great things it can do. However, if this is your first tablet, there are some essentials that you should be familiar with to get the most from the device. This chapter starts you off on the right foot by teaching you about the basic operation of the Kindle Fire.

The Hardware

Your Kindle Fire is equipped with a power button on the bottom of the device. Press and release this button to power on your Kindle Fire. If the Kindle Fire is already turned on, a quick press of the power button puts it to sleep. Pressing and holding the power button enables you to power off your Kindle Fire completely.

Should You Power Off?

The display on your Kindle Fire is the primary power consumer on the device. Therefore, your Kindle Fire uses much less power when it's in sleep mode. Turning it off completely obviously uses even less power, but if you subscribe to a magazine or a newspaper, you won't get your subscription automatically when your Kindle Fire is turned off.

To the left of the power button is a micro-USB port for charging your Kindle Fire. You can also use the micro-USB port to connect your Kindle Fire to a computer so that you can manually transfer files to the device. However, Amazon doesn't provide a micro-USB cable when you purchase a Kindle Fire, so you have to buy one separately if you want to connect the Kindle Fire to a computer.

Audio Plug   **Power Button**

Micro-USB Port

Charging over USB

When your Kindle Fire is plugged into your computer with a USB cable, the power button lights up orange as though the device were charging. However, the battery charges over USB only when the screen is turned off. If the screen is turned on, the battery drains even if the Kindle Fire is connected to a computer by USB cable.

When your Kindle Fire is charging, the power button illuminates with an orange glow. When your Kindle Fire is fully charged, the light turns green. Charging the Kindle Fire takes about four hours, and you can expect to get approximately eight hours of use from a full charge. However, if you play a lot of games or use the Wi-Fi connection a lot, you can expect fewer hours of use between charges.

To the left of the micro-USB port is a 1/4" audio plug for headphones or other audio devices, such as an external speaker set. The Kindle Fire is best suited for earbuds such as those that come with cell phones or portable music play-ers. If you have a high-quality set of headphones, you might want to use a portable headphone amplifier to improve the audio quality.

At the top of your Kindle Fire are two stereo speakers. These speakers are suit-able for basic sounds from your Kindle Fire, but for listening to music or watching videos, headphones or an external speaker set are definitely better options.

Speakers

One thing you might notice missing in the way of buttons is a volume con-trol. There aren't buttons on the Kindle Fire for controlling volume. Instead, you have to use the volume slider that is available in the Kindle Fire interface. See the "Adjusting the Volume" task later in this chapter for more information about controlling the volume.

Changing the Screen Timeout

Your Kindle Fire's screen turns off automatically after 5 minutes without use. You can adjust the timeout or you can turn the automatic timeout off completely.

1. Tap Quick Settings.

2. Tap More.

3. Tap Display.

4. Tap Screen Timeout.

5. Select a screen timeout.

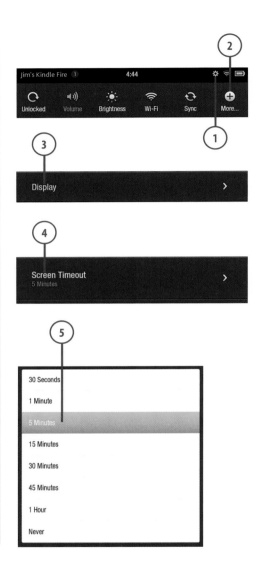

Initial Setup

When you first turn on your Kindle Fire, you see the lock screen. Swipe your finger in the direction of the colored arrow to unlock the device. You then go through a series of steps that get you started using your new device.

Connecting to a Listed Wi-Fi Network

In order to access content on your Kindle Fire, you need to connect to a Wi-Fi network, which is where the initial set-up process begins.

Manually Connecting to a Wi-Fi Network

If you need to return to the Wi-Fi setup, you can tap Quick Settings and then tap Wi-Fi.

1. Tap the name of your Wi-Fi network.

2. Enter the password for your Wi-Fi network.

3. Tap Connect.

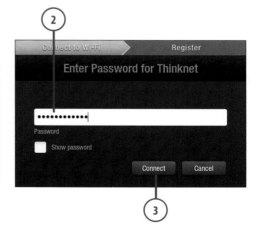

Connecting to an Unlisted Wi-Fi Network

If your network's name isn't listed, you might need to manually enter the information necessary to connect to your Wi-Fi network.

1. Tap Enter Other Wi-Fi Network.

2. Enter the name (SSID) of your network.

3. Tap the type of security that your network uses.

4. Enter the password for your network if necessary.

5. Tap Connect.

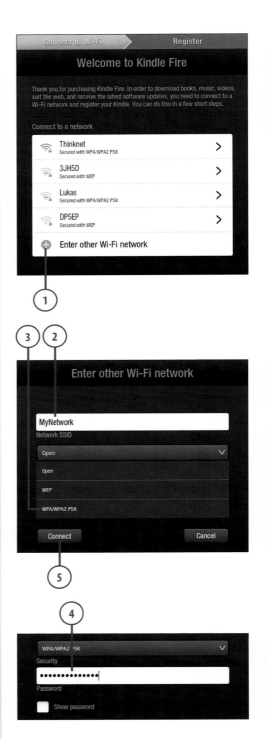

Setting Your Time Zone

Your Kindle Fire doesn't have a GPS, so it can't determine your time zone automatically. You need to select your time zone during setup.

1. Tap your time zone.

2. If your time zone isn't listed, tap Select Another Time Zone to see a list of additional time zones.

3. Tap Continue.

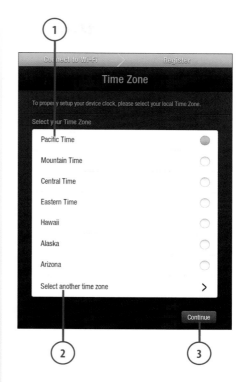

Registering with Amazon

Your Kindle Fire must be registered with an Amazon account so that you can access content. If your Kindle is not already registered to your Amazon account (often they're shipped already registered to the buyer's account), you need to do that next.

1. Enter your email address that is registered with Amazon.

2. Enter your Amazon password.

3. Tap Register.

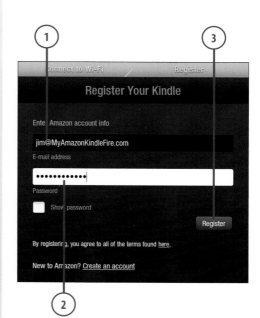

Don't Have an Amazon Account?

If you don't already have an Amazon account, you can create one online at Amazon.com or you can tap Create an Account to create one on your Kindle Fire.

Kindle Fire Updates

It's possible that your Kindle Fire won't have the latest version of the Kindle operating system. If it doesn't, the latest version is downloaded and installed automatically when you set up your Kindle Fire for the first time.

The final step in the initial setup is the Welcome screen. Tap Get Started Now to begin using your Kindle Fire. The Kindle Fire guides you through a series of screens that describe some of the basic usability features of the tablet.

Basic Usage of the Kindle Fire

By now you're already familiar with tapping to select buttons and other items on your Kindle Fire. You can also use several other gestures to interact with your Kindle Fire.

Canceling a Tap

Taps are registered when you lift your finger from the screen. If you tap something by mistake and you want to cancel the tap, slide your finger onto another part of the screen before lifting it.

In addition to tapping to select items, you can double-tap to do things such as zoom on a figure in a book or a website. To double-tap, tap your finger on the same point on the screen twice in quick succession.

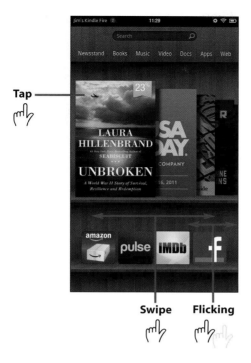

Tap

Swipe   **Flicking**

You can scroll through lists of items both horizontally and vertically by swiping your finger. Hold your finger on the list and move it up and down or left and right to scroll through items. To quickly scroll, flick your finger in the direction you want to scroll as you remove your finger from the screen.

To incrementally zoom in and out, you can use pinch and reverse pinch gestures. This is typically used on pictures, websites, and subscription content, but many applications also allow you to use this gesture.

To zoom in, place your thumb and index finger on the screen close together and move them apart (reverse pinching). To zoom out, place your thumb and index finger on the screen with some distance between them and move them together (pinching).

The Home Screen

After you complete the initial setup, your Kindle Fire automatically takes you to the main screen (called the Home screen). The Navigation menu provides quick access to the content libraries available on the Kindle Fire. The Carousel contains thumbnails for your books, subscription content, and recently accessed videos, music, and websites. Slide or flick across the Carousel to browse the items available there. Tapping an item opens that item. You can't change the order of items in the Carousel. The most recently accessed items will always appear first.

Easier Carousel Selection
You can tap on the right edge of any item that's visible and the Carousel immediately flips to that item. You can then tap it to select it.

Navigation menu

Carousel

Favorites shelf

Downloading Items

The Carousel displays both items on your Kindle Fire (called *device items*) and items that are in your online library (called *cloud items*). If you want to open a cloud item, you first need to download it to your device.

Identifying Cloud Items

Cloud items display a downward arrow in the lower-right when they are the topmost item in the carousel.

1. Swipe to the item you'd like to download. You see a downward-pointing arrow in the lower-right corner of the item.

2. Tap the item to download it to your device.

3. While the item is downloading, you can tap the X to cancel the download. Once an item has been downloaded, it is a device item and can be accessed at any time, even when not connected to Wi-Fi.

Removing Downloaded Items from Your Device

After an item is downloaded, it takes up some of the memory on your Kindle Fire. You only have 8GB of memory for storage of downloaded items, so you can free up some memory by removing unused items from your device. Removing an item from the device only removes the downloaded copy. The item is still available to you in your cloud library.

1. Tap and hold on the item you'd like to remove.

2. Tap Remove from Device.

Cloud Versus Device

"Cloud" is a common buzz phrase in today's technology. If something is in the cloud, it means that it exists on a computer that you access via the Internet instead of on your local device. The Kindle Fire accesses a lot of its content on Amazon's computers in the cloud.

Many screens on the Kindle Fire enable you to choose whether you are viewing content on the device or in the cloud. Having content in the cloud makes it easy to share that content between multiple devices.

Adding an Item to Favorites

The Favorites shelf is located below the carousel. It provides a convenient way for you to access your most often used items. You can add any item to Favorites.

Tip

By default, there are two Favorites shelves. However, as you add items to Favorites, your Kindle Fire adds additional shelves as needed. You can swipe up and down to browse the Favorites shelves.

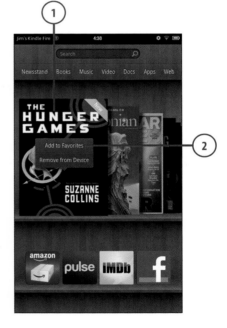

1. Tap and hold on the item you want to add to Favorites.

2. Tap Add to Favorites.

Adding Subscription Items to Favorites

If you add a subscription item to Favorites and that item isn't currently on your device, the item is downloaded immediately. If you remove that item from your device at a later time, it is automatically removed from Favorites as well.

Removing an Item from Favorites

If you decide you no longer want an item to be listed in Favorites, you can remove it.

1. Tap and hold on the item in Favorites.

2. Tap Remove from Favorites.

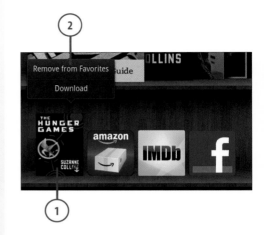

Rearranging Favorites

By default, items are listed in Favorites in the order in which you add them. If you'd like to rearrange your Favorites, you can easily do so.

1. Tap and hold on the item you'd like to move.

2. Drag the item to the new location.

3. Release the item.

Notifications and Options

The Status Bar appears at the top of most Kindle Fire screens. The Status Bar displays the name of your Kindle Fire, a notification indicator (if notifications are present), the clock, the Quick Settings button, the Wi-Fi signal indicator, and the battery meter.

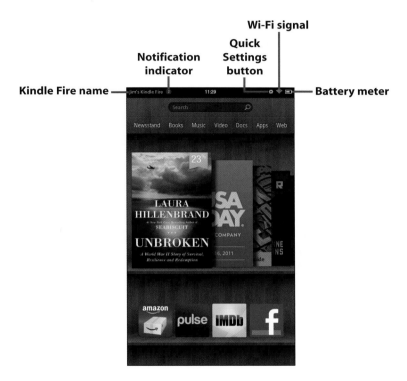

Notifications

Your Kindle Fire uses the notification indicator to inform you of any background tasks and other important information that's going on behind the scenes. When you see the notification indicator, you can tap it to get more information.

1. Tap the notification indicator.

2. Tap a notification for more information or additional options.

Value of Notifications

Notifications might not be very obvious from the Home screen, but the information and options they provide is often valuable. I cover specific notifications that you should pay special attention to throughout the book.

Options

The Options bar appears at the bottom of most screens. The buttons on the Options Bar are called icons and include a Home icon, a Back icon, a Menu icon, and a Search icon on most screens. The Home icon always takes you to the Home screen. The Back icon takes you back one screen, the Menu icon displays a menu for the current screen, and the Search icon displays the Search screen.

Home icon   Menu icon

Back icon   Search icon

Other Options Bar Icons

Depending on the screen, you might see additional icons on the Options bar. These are covered throughout the book where they're applicable.

Settings

I cover many of the Kindle Fire's settings throughout the book as necessary, but there are some general settings that you should be familiar with immediately.

Locking the Screen Orientation

Your Kindle Fire features an accelerometer that can sense the orientation of the device. When you turn the device while holding it, the screen rotates automatically to match the orientation of the device. In some cases, you might want to prevent the screen from rotating. For example, if you're reading a web page in portrait mode, setting your Kindle Fire on a table will sometimes flip the orientation. You can lock the orientation to prevent this.

Orientation Isn't Always Your Choice

If you are watching videos, your Kindle Fire will switch to landscape orientation automatically.

1. With the screen displaying the desired orientation, tap Quick Settings.

2. Tap Unlocked to lock the orientation. The label on the icon changes to Locked.

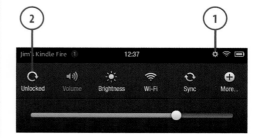

Adjusting the Volume

There are no hard buttons for adjusting the volume on your Kindle Fire. You adjust volume using an onscreen slider.

1. Tap Quick Settings.

2. If the volume control isn't visible, tap Volume.

3. Slide the volume control to the right to increase volume and to the left to decrease volume.

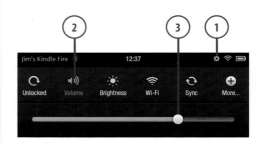

Adjusting Screen Brightness

As mentioned earlier, the screen on the Kindle Fire uses more power than anything else, and the brighter the screen, the more battery power it uses. To increase battery life, you can lower the brightness of the display.

1. Tap Quick Settings.

2. Tap Brightness.

3. Slide the brightness control to the right to increase brightness and to the left to decrease brightness.

Checking Device Information

The Device screen displays information about your Kindle Fire, such as the percentage of battery remaining, how much storage space you've used, the version of your operating system, and other useful information.

1. Tap Quick Settings.

2. Tap More.

3. Tap Device.

4. The Device screen displays.

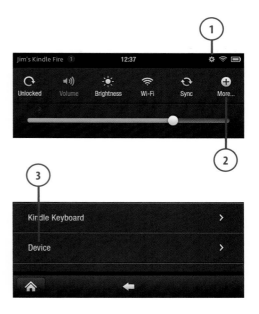

Turning Off Wi-Fi

There may be occasions where you need to turn off your Kindle Fire's Wi-Fi radio, such as when you're traveling on commercial flights and in other sensitive areas. Turning Wi-Fi off also consumes less battery power when you're just kicking back and reading.

1. Tap Quick Settings.

2. Tap Wi-Fi.

3. Tap Off to turn off Wi-Fi.

4. Tap On to turn Wi-Fi on again.

Searches

All of the content in your Kindle library is indexed for easy searching. Search is more useful than it might at first seem. For example, when you're reading a novel, you can use search to find references to a particular character. This is particularly helpful when you pick up a partially read book that you haven't read in a while.

Search results include content both on your device and in the cloud.

Searching Within Content

You can also search within books and other content. I cover how to do that in the Searching Content section of Chapter 3, "Reading on the Kindle Fire."

Searching Your Library

Searching your library returns results from books, periodicals, music, documents, and apps.

1. From the Home screen, tap inside the search box.

2. Tap Library to search your library.

3. Enter the text you'd like to search for using the keyboard that appears at the bottom of the screen. Results appear as you type.

4. Tap the item to either download the item or go to the item.

Searching the Web

In addition to searching for items in your library, you can also search the Web quickly from the Home screen.

1. From the Home screen, tap inside the search box.

2. Tap Web to search the Web.

3. Enter the text you'd like to search for. Results appear as you type.

4. Tap an item in the results to open a search page using your default search engine.

Changing Your Web Search Engine

I cover how you can change your default web search engine in Chapter 10, "Browsing the Web with Silk," when we talk about the Kindle Fire's web browser.

The Kindle Fire Keyboard

Your Kindle Fire's keyboard is much like the keyboard you use on your computer. However, unlike your computer's keyboard, there are obviously no physical keys. Instead, your Kindle Fire's keyboard uses touch just like the rest of the interface.

At first, you might find the Kindle Fire's keyboard a bit hard to get used to, but after some time, you'll find it to be an easy way to enter data. In fact, there are some features that the Kindle Fire's keyboard provides that you won't find on your computer.

Entering Text

Entering text using your Kindle Fire's keyboard is a simple task, and there are a few convenient features to make it easier.

1. Tap an area where text entry is possible.

2. Tap letters on the keyboard to enter your text.

3. Tap a suggested word to insert the word.

4. Tap the Keyboard icon to dismiss the keyboard if you need to see what's behind it.

Dismissing the Keyboard

In some cases, the Home icon or the Back icon might be hidden by the keyboard. In those cases, you'll need to tap the Keyboard icon to dismiss the keyboard.

A Couple of Shortcuts

You can quickly add a period to the end of a sentence by double-tapping the space key.

You can activate caps lock by double-tapping the Shift key.

Positioning the Cursor and Selecting Text

As you type, characters are added at the position of the cursor. You can reposition the cursor if necessary.

1. Tap in the text entry area.

2. Tap and hold on the cursor indicator.

3. Drag the cursor indicator to a new position and release it.

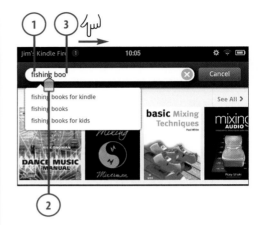

Selecting and Editing Text

You might need to select some or all of the text you've entered in order to change it or remove it.

1. Double-tap the entered text.

2. Drag the left indicator to the beginning of your desired selection.

3. Drag the right indicator to the end of your desired selection.

4. Press Backspace to delete the section or type to replace the selection.

Copy/Cut and Paste

You might find that you want to copy or cut some text and then paste it somewhere else. For example, you might want to copy some text from one email message and paste it into another.

1. Tap and hold on the text you want to copy.

2. Tap Select Word or Select All.

3. Drag the selection handles to highlight text you want to copy.

4. Tap and hold on the selected text.

5. Tap Copy or Cut.

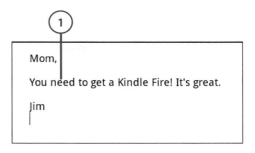

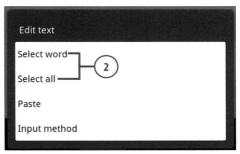

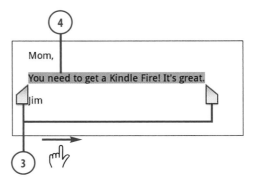

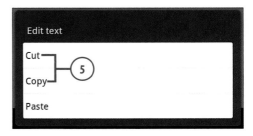

6. Tap and hold where you want to paste the text you copied.

7. Tap Paste.

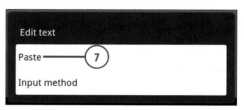

Entering Punctuation and Numbers

Punctuation and numbers can be entered by using the number key.

1. Tap the number key to change the keyboard so that it displays numbers and punctuation marks.

2. Tap a number or punctuation mark to enter it.

3. Tap the symbol key to switch the keyboard to symbol mode.

4. Tap a symbol to enter it.

There's an easier way to enter punctuation and numbers.

1. Tap and hold a letter on the top
   row.

2. Slide your finger to highlight the
   desired character and release.

3. Tap and hold on the period key to
   display punctuation characters.

4. Slide your finger to highlight the
   desired character and release.

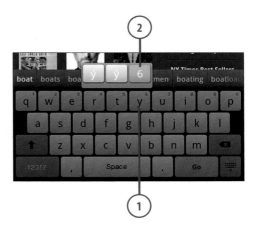

Hidden Characters

Tap and hold on other keyboard
keys to reveal shortcuts to other
special characters. Unfortunately,
there often isn't any way to know
if a key has hidden characters by
simply looking at the key.

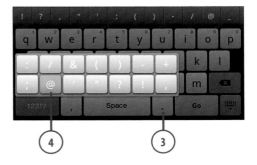

Instant Video

Cloud Player and
Cloud Drive

Cloud Reader

In this chapter, you learn about Amazon's cloud services that make your Kindle Fire more enjoyable.

→ Amazon Cloud Drive
→ Amazon Cloud Player
→ Amazon Instant Video
→ Kindle Cloud Reader

Amazon's Cloud Services

Amazon offers a collection of cloud services that augment the functionality of the Kindle Fire. In fact, your Kindle Fire is designed to be a handheld conduit into these cloud services. You can set up a cloud drive, add all of your music, and that music is immediately available to you on your Kindle Fire anywhere you can connect to Wi-Fi. You can get a movie or TV show from Amazon on your computer or set-top box, watch part of it on your television, and then pick right up to watch the rest on your Kindle Fire while in bed or while traveling. You may as well think of your Kindle Fire as a window into the world of Amazon's cloud services.

Amazon Cloud Drive

Your computer has a hard drive in it where you can store your stuff. When you're sitting at your computer, that stuff is easy to access, but what about when you're not at your computer? If you have Internet access, that's when cloud storage comes in handy. The cloud is just another word for the Internet, so when you have something stored in the cloud, you can access it from anyplace where you have Internet access.

Amazon provides 5GB of free storage that you can use for music, pictures, videos, or anything else you want to store in the cloud. You can buy additional storage for a nominal fee.

While your Kindle Fire's Music screen does provide access to your music stored in the cloud, you'll need to use Silk (the Kindle Fire's web browser) to view other file types stored in your Cloud Drive.

Unlimited Space for Music

As of this writing, if you purchase any paid Cloud Drive plan for as little as $20 per year, Amazon gives you unlimited space for music files, whether purchased from Amazon or not.

Accessing Your Cloud Drive

You can access your Cloud Drive using Silk on your Kindle Fire or using the web browser on your computer.

1. Open your web browser and browse to www.amazon.com.

2. Point to Amazon Cloud Drive.

3. Select Your Cloud Drive from the menu.

4. Enter your email address and your Amazon password if prompted.

After you log in, you'll see your Cloud Drive and a big Upload button if you haven't uploaded any files yet. I'll show you how to create folders and upload files next.

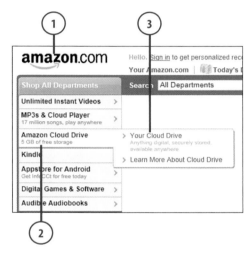

Creating Folders

By default, your Cloud Drive contains folders for common file types. You'll see folders for music, pictures, documents, and so forth. Those folders are a good starting point, but you might want to create additional folders. For example, if you're uploading pictures from a recent family vacation, you might want to create a folder inside of the Pictures folder called *Family Vacation* and upload your pictures there.

1. Click New Folder.

2. Enter a name for the folder.

3. Click Save Folder.

More Actions
You can copy, move, and rename files and folders using the More Actions button.

Deleting a Folder

You can delete folders from your Cloud Drive that you no longer need or to free up some space.

1. Click Your Cloud Drive so that your folders are visible.

2. Check the box to the left of the folder(s) you want to delete.

3. Click Delete.

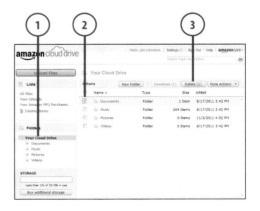

Deleted Files

If you delete a folder that contains files, the files are deleted along with the folder. If you accidentally delete your files, you can recover them from Deleted Items. Files in Deleted Items remain there until you permanently delete them, and they continue to use space in your cloud drive. To permanently delete them, click the Permanently Delete button in Deleted Items.

Recovering Deleted Items

You can recover folders that you've accidentally deleted. Recovering a folder also recovers the files that were originally inside the folder.

1. Click Deleted Items.

2. Check the box to the left of the folder(s) you want to recover.

3. Click Restore to Folder.

Adding Files to Your Cloud Drive

To add files to your Cloud Drive, you upload them to Amazon.

1. Click the Upload Files button near the top left corner of the Cloud Drive screen.

2. Click the drop-down to select a folder for your uploaded files.

3. Select your folder and click Select.

4. Click Select Files to Upload.

5. Select one or more files for upload.

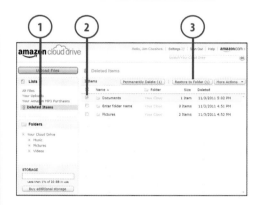

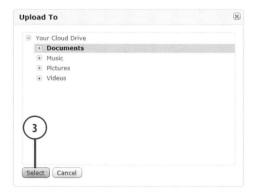

Uploading Music Files

If you're uploading music files, you can use Amazon Cloud Player to upload more easily using Amazon's MP3 Uploader. Click the Amazon Cloud Player link in the Upload Files dialog in step 2.

Music that you upload to your Cloud Drive can be streamed or downloaded from the Music screen on your Kindle Fire. Other files in your Cloud Drive are accessible using Silk.

Downloading Files from Your Cloud Drive

You can download one file at a time from your Cloud Drive.

1. Navigate to the file you want to download by clicking the folder that contains the file.

2. Place a check in the box to the left of the file you want to download.

3. Click Download.

4. Select the folder where you want to save the file.

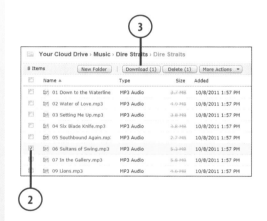

Downloading Music Files

If you would like to download multiple music files, use Amazon Cloud Player, which only allows for the download of music files and provides a better interface for doing so.

Amazon Cloud Player

Amazon Cloud Player is a convenient way to listen to music on your Cloud Drive when you don't have your Kindle Fire with you. You can use Cloud Player on a computer or on most mobile devices.

Albums/Artists

Your Music

Songs

Play Controls   **Now Playing**

Launching Cloud Player

Amazon Cloud Player is available as an Android application if you have an Android phone. If not, you can access the Cloud Player from your web browser. While you can use Silk to access Cloud Player, it doesn't really make sense to do so because the Music screen provides access to your Cloud Drive music.

1. Open your web browser and browse to www.amazon.com.

2. Point to MP3s and Cloud Player on the menu.

3. Click on Cloud Player for Web.

4. If prompted, enter your email address and Amazon password.

>>> *Go Further*

UPLOADING YOUR MUSIC

You can easily upload your music to Amazon Cloud Player. Click Upload Your Music in the upper left of the Cloud Player to download the Amazon MP3 Uploader. Music that you upload must be in either MP3 or unprotected AAC (iTunes) format. If your music is in some other format, you can find free converters by searching the Internet, but my preferred MP3 converter is dbPowerAmp, available from www.dbpoweramp.com/dmc.htm. Music that you purchase from Amazon's MP3 Music Store is automatically added to your Cloud Drive by default and does not require a Cloud Drive subscription plan.

Playing Music

You can stream music from Cloud Player without downloading the music to your computer.

1. Locate the music you want to play. You can browse by song, artist, album, or genre.

2. Click the checkbox next to one or more songs to select the songs to play. You can also check the box at the top of the list to select all songs that are displayed.

3. Click the Play button.

4. To go to the next song, click the Next button.

5. To go to the previous song, click the Previous button.

Shuffle and Repeat Songs

You can shuffle or repeat the songs you are playing by clicking the Repeat or Random button under the large Play button in the lower-left corner of Cloud Player.

Creating Playlists

You can create playlists of songs in order to play only the songs you want to hear. Playlists are a great way to make a song list for a party or special event. Playlists you create in Cloud Player are also available on your Kindle Fire.

Refreshing Cloud Drive

Your Cloud Drive on your Kindle Fire refreshes every 10 minutes. Songs or playlists that you add will appear once a refresh occurs.

1. Select the songs you want to add to your playlist.

2. Click the Add to Playlist button.

3. If you haven't created a playlist yet, enter a name for a new playlist. Otherwise, choose New Playlist or an existing playlist for the selected songs.

4. Browse to other songs and add them to your playlist as desired.

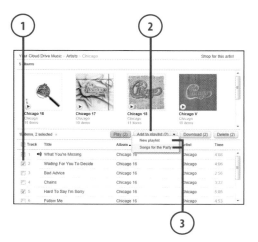

Downloading Songs to a Computer

If you plan on being away from an Internet connection, you can still play your music by first downloading it to your computer.

1. Select the songs you want to download.

2. Click the Download button. If you don't already have the Amazon MP3 Downloader, you are asked to download and install it.

3. Your browser prompts you to open or save a file with an .amz file extension. Select the option to open the file.

4. The MP3 Downloader launches, downloads your files, and imports them into iTunes or Windows Media Player on your computer.

CHANGING MP3 DOWNLOADER OPTIONS

Go Further

The MP3 Downloader will detect if you have iTunes installed. If you do, after it downloads a song, it automatically imports that song into iTunes. You can change this behavior, and you can also change the folder where MP3 Downloader saves the songs you download.

To change MP3 Downloader options, click File, Preferences. You can click the Change button to choose to save your songs to a different folder. You can also select what the MP3 Downloader should do with a song after you download it.

Change Button

It's best to change these settings before you start downloading songs. You can find the MP3 Downloader on your PC in the Amazon folder on your Start menu. On the Mac, you can locate it using the Finder.

Changing How Amazon Handles Purchased Music

You can choose whether Amazon automatically adds music that you buy from Amazon's MP3 Music Store to your Cloud Drive. You can also choose whether or not music added to your Cloud Drive automatically is downloaded to your computer.

1. Click Settings from the Amazon Cloud Player.

2. Select Your Amazon MP3 Settings.

3. Select whether songs are saved to your Amazon Cloud Drive or saved to a device. If you choose Save to Device, purchases download to your computer and are not saved to your Cloud Drive.

4. If you choose to save music to your Cloud Drive automatically, you can also choose whether or not music added to your Cloud Drive is downloaded to your computer.

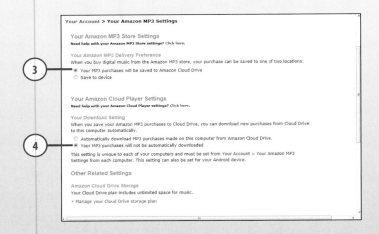

Settings Are Instant and Per Computer

Changes you make to your Amazon MP3 options take effect immediately and are unique to the computer you are using when you set them. If you want your options to take effect on all computers, you need to change them explicitly on each computer you use.

Amazon Instant Video

Amazon has a huge selection of videos, including both movies and television programs, that you can watch on your Kindle Fire, but you can also watch those videos on your computer. You can also purchase or rent videos on your computer and watch them on your Kindle Fire or vice versa.

Getting Videos from Amazon Instant Video

You can use your computer to buy, rent, or stream Amazon Instant Video. Videos that you buy or rent are available on your computer, on your Kindle Fire, or on any other device that supports Amazon Instant Video.

If you're an Amazon Prime subscriber, you have access to more than 10,000 videos that you can stream instantly at no additional charge to your computer, TV, or Kindle Fire.

Free Prime for Caregivers

If you're a primary caregiver (mom, dad, grandparent, and so forth) for a young child, you can get Prime free by joining Amazon Mom. Browse to www.amazon.com/prime for details.

1. Open your web browser and browse to www.amazon.com/instantvideo.

2. Select the movie or TV show that you want to watch.

3. Choose to purchase, rent, or watch your video. Not all options are available for all titles.

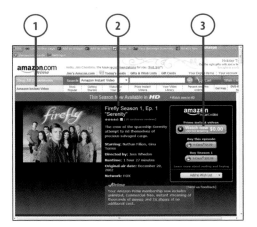

Why Rent or Buy Instead of Stream Free Prime Video?

If you're an Amazon Prime member, you may be able to watch a title free, but you still may want to rent it instead. Why? If you want to watch on your Kindle Fire and you don't have Wi-Fi access, you need to first download the movie or TV show. You can only download videos that you've either purchased or rented.

If you rent a video, you have 30 days to begin watching it before it expires. After you begin watching it, you have 48 hours to complete it before the rental expires.

Kindle Cloud Reader

The Kindle Cloud Reader makes it possible to read your Kindle books in your web browser from any location with Internet access. Kindle Cloud Reader requires either Google Chrome (www.google.com/chrome), Apple Safari (www.apple.com/safari), or Firefox version 6 or higher (www.getfirefox.com).

Accessing Kindle Cloud Reader

1. Browse to read.amazon.com using the Chrome, Safari, or Firefox web browsers.

iSafari

If you have an iPhone, an iPad, or an iPod touch, you can use Safari on that device to use Kindle Cloud Reader. By using Cloud Reader on your device, you can shop for Kindle books from within the integrated store, something that's not possible with the Kindle app for iOS.

2. Click the Sign In to Get Started button.

3. Enter your email address and your Amazon password.

4. If you want to be able to continue reading in Kindle Cloud Reader without an Internet connection, click Enable Offline to enable offline reading.

5. Click Continue to install Cloud Reader.

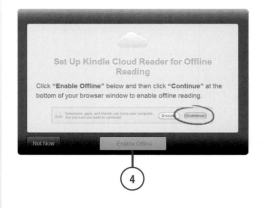

6. Click the Cloud Reader app in your browser.

7. Click the Get Started Now button to start using Kindle Cloud Reader.

Cloud Button shows books in the cloud.

Downloaded Button shows books you've downloaded to your computer.

Opening and Downloading Books

You can read books that are in the cloud (stored on Amazon's computers) or that are downloaded to your own computer. Only books that you've downloaded to your own computer can be read without an Internet connection.

1. Locate the book you'd like to read. You can click the magnifying glass at the top of the screen to search for books if necessary.

2. Click on a book to start reading it. If you want to download a book for offline reading right-click the book and click Download & Pin Book.

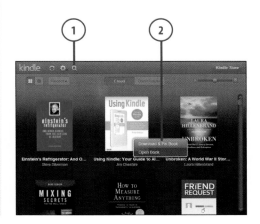

Downloaded Books

Downloaded books are accessible by clicking the Downloaded button at the top of the screen, but they're also visible when Kindle Cloud Reader's Cloud button is pressed. Downloaded books display a green pin under the book's cover.

After you download your first book, Cloud Reader downloads other books that you read automatically. These books are automatically deleted periodically. If you want to ensure that a downloaded book isn't automatically deleted, right-click it and choose Download & Pin Book.

Reading Books

Cloud Reader has many of the same reading features you find in the Kindle Fire.

1. Open a book as described in the previous section. If the book has been opened previously on any Kindle device, it automatically opens at the furthest point read.

2. To turn pages, use the arrow keys on your keyboard or click the arrows on the left and right sides of the page.

3. Quickly access a part of the book using the Go To menu.

4. Change font size, margins, and color settings using the View Settings button.

5. Bookmark a page using the Bookmark button.

6. Synchronize with your other Kindle devices using the Synchronize button.

7. View notes and highlights using the Toggle Notes and Marks button.

8. Click the Library button to return to your library.

Notes and Marks

You cannot create notes and highlights in Cloud Reader, but you can view notes and marks created on your Kindle Fire or other Kindle device or app.

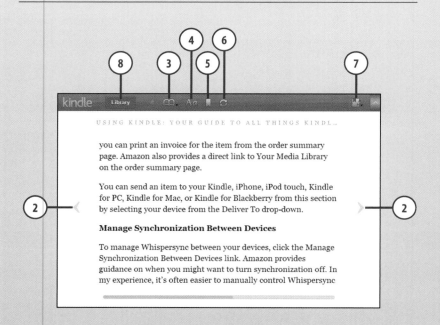

Set Bookmarks

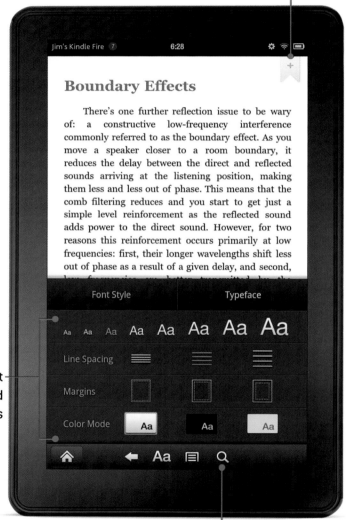

Change Font Styles and Colors

Search Your Content

In this chapter, you learn about ways that you can find content for your Kindle Fire and how to read and interact with that content. You also find out how you can search your Kindle Fire libraries.

Reading on the Kindle Fire

Your Kindle Fire is a great tablet computer, but it's still a Kindle eBook reader at heart. Its smaller size makes it convenient to carry with you so that you can read your books, magazines, newspapers, and other content no matter where you are.

Finding Content

Amazon's Kindle Store provides access to a huge assortment of reading content for your Kindle Fire. You can find just about any book you want to read for the Kindle, many at deeply discounted prices. In addition to books, Amazon offers a wide array of newspapers and magazines as well, and because your Kindle Fire's screen is full-color, reading periodicals on a Kindle is a pleasurable experience.

Your source of great content doesn't stop with Amazon. You can also check out books from your local library, borrow books from friends and family, and even download books from other online eBook stores and websites and then transfer them to your Kindle Fire.

Subscribing to Periodicals

The Kindle Store offers a wide array of newspapers and magazines, including some that are optimized with multimedia content specifically for the Kindle Fire.

1. From the Home screen, tap Newsstand to open the Newsstand.

2. Tap Store to open the Kindle Newsstand.

Easy Return to the Storefront

While you're browsing in the Newsstand, you can easily return to the storefront by tapping Newsstand to the left of the search box.

3. Choose a magazine or newspaper you'd like to read.

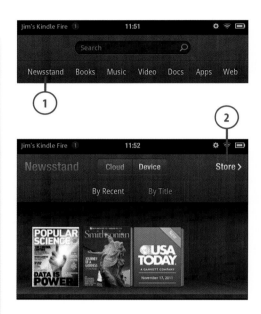

4. Tap Subscribe Now to download the latest edition to your Kindle Fire or Buy Current Issue to buy and download the current issue.

Trial Subscriptions

Most periodicals provide a 14-day trial subscription during which time you are not charged. Unless you cancel your subscription within the 14-days, you are charged beginning on the 15th day.

Canceling Subscriptions

If you want to cancel a subscrip-tion, you need to use Amazon's Manage Your Kindle page. Read about the Manage Your Kindle page in Chapter 4, "Using Amazon's Manage Your Kindle Page."

Sampling and Buying Books

Amazon's Kindle Store has more than 1 million books, and they're all avail-able to you with your Kindle Fire.

1. From the Home screen, tap Books.

2. Tap Store.

3. Tap a book that you'd like to read on your Kindle Fire.

4. Tap Try a Sample to download a sample of the book. Sample lengths vary based on the book.

5. Tap Buy to purchase the book and add it to your Kindle library.

6. Tap Borrow for Free to borrow the book if you are an Amazon Prime member.

Can't Borrow

If a book is not available for borrowing, the Borrow for Free button won't be visible. If you've already borrowed a book during the last month, the Borrow for Free button is grayed out like the one shown here.

Finding My Books

After you buy a book or download a sample from the Kindle Store, it appears on the Books screen and in the Carousel on the Home screen.

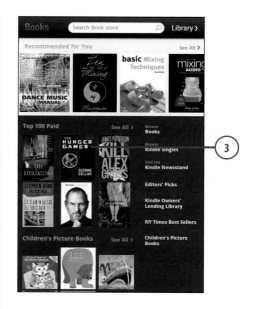

Borrowing Books from Amazon

You can borrow one book per month from Amazon's Kindle Owners' Lending Library. You can keep borrowed books as long as you'd like, but you can only borrow one book at a time.

Check Out Your Local Library

You can also check out Kindle books from thousands of local libraries across the United States. To find out if your local library offers this service, go to www.overdrive.com and enter your ZIP code.

The Amazon Kindle Owners' Lending Library contains approximately 5,000 books and is available only to Amazon Prime members.

1. From the Home screen, tap Books.

2. Tap Store to open the Kindle Store.

3. If a book is available for borrowing for Prime members, tap Borrow for Free to borrow the book and add it to your library.

Finding Prime Books

To find books that are available in the Kindle Owners' Lending Library, tap Kindle Owners' Lending Library on the home page of the Kindle store.

Only on Kindle Devices

Books borrowed from the Kindle Lending Library can only be read on a Kindle device. You cannot read them on the Kindle app on any other device.

Lending Books to Friends and Family

Some books can be lent to friends or family. Your friend or family member isn't required to have a Kindle device to read the book you lend to them. Loaned books can be read on a computer or other device with the free Kindle application.

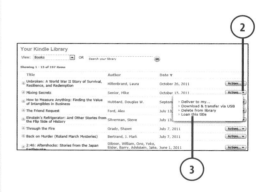

1. Open your web browser and browse to www.amazon.com/manageyourkindle.

2. Hover your mouse pointer over the Actions drop-down next to the title you would like to lend.

3. Click Loan This Title.

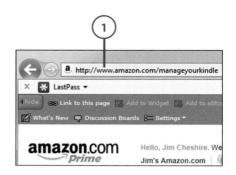

Why Can't I Lend My Book?

It's up to the publisher of a book to decide whether or not the book can be loaned to others. If a publisher hasn't granted that right for a particular book, the option to lend the book is not available.

You can find out if a book can be loaned to others by reviewing the Product Details for the book on Amazon's site. If the book can be loaned, it will display "Lending: Enabled.

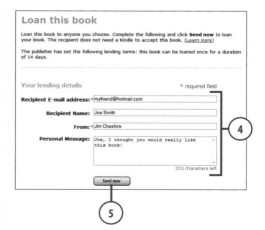

4. Enter your friend or family member's information and a personal message.

5. Click Send Now.

What Happens Next?

When you lend a book, the recipient of the book receives an email with a link to accept the request. He or she needs an Amazon account, but a Kindle device is not necessary to borrow a Kindle book.

You are not able to read a book while it is loaned out to someone. You can see the status of the loan on the Manage Your Kindle page at www.amazon.com/manageyourkindle.

Sideloading Books

There are many sources of eBooks, many of which are free. (An Internet search for "free Kindle books" turns up plenty of sources.) After you download a Kindle-compatible eBook, you can transfer it to your Kindle using the USB cable. Manually transferring books from your computer to your Kindle is called *sideloading*. Sideloaded books are available in the Docs library on your Kindle.

An Easier Way to Sideload Books

A better way to sideload books and manage your Kindle content is to use Calibre. Calibre can even convert eBooks in non-Kindle formats to a Kindle-compatible format automatically, and these converted books will show up in the Books screen instead of the Docs screen. See Chapter 5, "Managing Content with Calibre," for details.

1. Plug your Kindle Fire into your computer using a micro-USB cable.

2. Open (double-click) the Kindle drive on your computer.

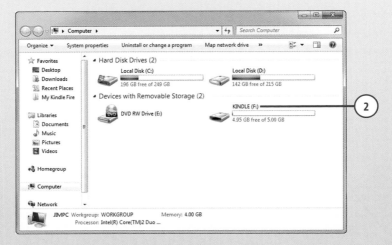

3. Select a book on your computer that you want to copy to your Kindle Fire and drag and drop it to either the Documents folder or the Books folder on your Kindle.

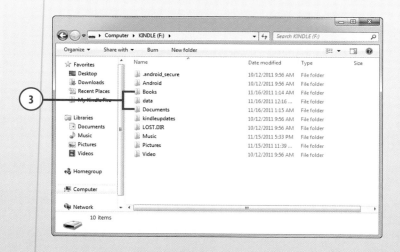

Reconnecting USB

If you tap Disconnect while your Kindle Fire is connected to your computer, you are no longer able to see the Kindle's folders on your computer. You can easily reconnect your Kindle by either unplugging the USB cable and plugging it back in or by tapping the Notification area of the Kindle and tapping the USB Is Connected notification.

Reading Books

The Kindle has always been a great device for reading. Instead of carrying around a bag of books, you can put all the books you would want to read on your Kindle. You can easily look up definitions with the integrated dictionary. You can search the Web when you want to read more about something you encounter in a book. You can even increase the size of a book's text to make it easier to read.

All of these great features are available on your Kindle Fire, and because it's a tablet computer, your Kindle Fire makes using these features easier than any other Kindle.

Browsing Your Library

You can view books on your device and in the cloud using the Books library.

1. From the Home screen, tap Books to access your Books library.

2. Tap Device to see content that has been downloaded to your Kindle Fire or Cloud to see content that is in your online library.

3. Tap By Author, By Recent, or By Title to change the order in which your books are sorted.

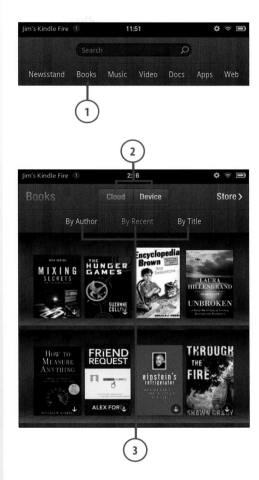

Downloading a Book to Your Device

Before you can read a book, you must first download it to your device.

1. From the Books library, tap Cloud to see the books in your online library.

Cloud and Device

When you are in Cloud view, you see books that are also on your device. That's because even after you download a book to your device, it is still in the cloud so that you can download it to other Kindles or devices.

Books in the cloud that haven't been downloaded to your device have a downward-pointing arrow in the lower-right corner.

2. Scroll to the book you want to download to your device.

3. Tap the book to download it to your device. You can also tap and hold the book and then tap Download.

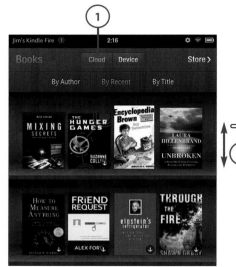

Removing a Book from Your Device

You can remove downloaded books from your Kindle Fire in order to free up some memory on the device.

1. From the Books library, tap Device to see the books on your device.

2. Scroll to the book that you want to remove from your device.

3. Tap and hold the book.

4. Tap Remove from Device.

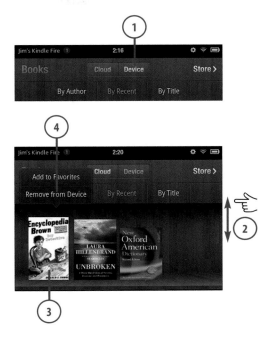

Reading a Book

The Kindle Fire is a great device for reading, and because it has a backlit screen, you can easily read in bed at night and in other low-light conditions without a reading light.

1. From the Books library, tap a book on your device to open it for reading.

My Book Doesn't Open on Page One

Kindle books open at the beginning of the book, but the beginning isn't necessarily page one. The publisher of a book can choose any page as the beginning of a book. Books frequently open at a point after the foreword, dedication, and other such sections.

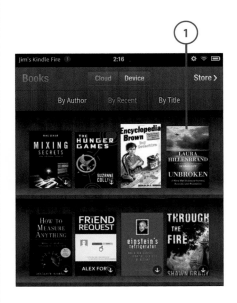

Books Aren't Only in the Library

You can also open a book for reading from the Carousel or the Favorites shelf.

2. Tap the right side of a page or swipe from right to left to move forward one page.

3. Tap the left side of a page or swipe from left to right to move back one page.

4. Tap the center of the page and swipe the Location slider to move to a specific location within the book.

Navigating a Book

You can tap the Menu icon for options to navigate to the cover, the table of content, or the beginning of a book. You can also enter a specific location number to quickly move to that location.

Because the Kindle Fire re-pages content based on the text size you use, it doesn't currently list actual page numbers. Amazon might add that feature in a future version of the Kindle Fire operating system.

UNBROKEN: A WORLD WAR II STORY OF SURVIVAL, RESILIENCE, AND RE...

Fourteen

Thirst

Pᴴɪʟ ꜰᴇʟᴛ ᴀꜱ ɪꜰ ʜᴇ ᴡᴇʀᴇ ᴏɴ ꜰɪʀᴇ. ᴛʜᴇ Eǫᴜᴀᴛᴏʀɪᴀʟ ꜱᴜɴ ʟᴀʏ upon the men, scalding their skin. Their upper lips burned and cracked, ballooning so dramatically that they obstructed their nostrils, while their lower lips bulged against their chins. Their bodies were slashed with open cracks that formed under the corrosive onslaught of sun, salt, wind, and fuel residue. Whitecaps slapped into the fissures, a sensation that Louie compared to having alcohol poured onto a wound. Sunlight glared off the ocean, sending barbs of white light into the men's pupils and leaving their heads pounding. The men's feet were cratered with quarter-sized salt sores. The rafts baked along with their occupants, emitting a bitter smell.

The water cans were empty. Desperately thirsty and overheated, the men could do no more than use their hands to bail seawater over themselves. The coolness of the ocean beckoned and couldn't be answered, for the sharks circled. One shark, six or eight feet long, stalked the rafts without rest, day and night. The men became especially wary of him, and when he ventured too close, one of them would

Pᴴɪʟ ꜰᴇʟᴛ ᴀꜱ ɪꜰ ʜᴇ ᴡᴇʀᴇ ᴏɴ ꜰɪʀᴇ. ᴛʜᴇ Eǫᴜᴀᴛᴏʀɪᴀʟ ꜱᴜɴ ʟᴀʏ upon the men, scalding their skin. Their upper lips burned and cracked, ballooning so dramatically that they obstructed their nostrils, while their lower lips bulged against their chins. Their bodies were slashed with open cracks that formed under the corrosive onslaught of sun, salt, wind, and fuel residue. Whitecaps slapped into the fissures, a sensation that Louie compared to having alcohol poured onto a wound. Sunlight glared off the ocean, sending barbs of white light into the men's pupils and leaving their heads pounding. The men's feet were cratered with quarter-sized salt sores. The rafts baked along with their occupants, emitting a bitter smell.

The water cans were empty. Desperately thirsty and overheated, the men could do no more than use their hands to bail seawater over themselves. The coolness of the ocean beckoned and couldn't be answered, for the sharks circled. One shark, six or

Location 2382 of 9328 • 25%

>>>Go Further

E INK VERSUS LCD

The Kindle comes in two flavors; the E Ink Kindles and the Kindle Fire. E Ink screens look very much like a printed page. They are easy to read, and because they don't rely on a backlight, you can read an E Ink display in bright sunlight just as you can a printed page. However, if you're like me and you want to read in bed, you'll need a light to read an E Ink display. Just like an actual book, an E Ink display doesn't provide its own illumination.

An LCD display can be read in darkness without a supplemental light source. However, many people feel that reading an LCD screen is irritating to the eyes. In my opinion, reading for several hours on an LCD screen can be fatiguing, but because the Kindle Fire's screen is not as large as a computer monitor or a large tablet, it's less tiring for me to read on it.

Perhaps the biggest drawback to an LCD screen is that it can't be read comfortably in bright sunlight. Even the best LCD screens are washed out in bright daylight, and your Kindle Fire suffers from that same drawback. Don't expect to spend much time reading your Kindle Fire while relaxing on the beach.

Looking Up Definitions

Your Kindle Fire comes with *The New Oxford American Dictionary* so that you can look up definitions of words while you're reading.

1. Tap and hold the word you want to look up in the dictionary. A definition of the word displays.

2. Tap the definition pop-up to dismiss it.

3. Tap Full Definition to open the dictionary and see a more detailed definition.

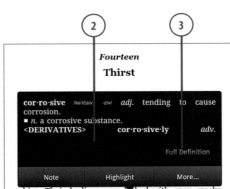

Returning from a Full Definition

To return to your book after viewing a full definition, tap the center of the screen and then tap the Back icon.

Definitions Are Not Just in Books

Definitions are available from books, magazines, newspapers, and in your personal documents.

Changing Font Styles

You can change the size of fonts, line spacing, page margins, and colors when reading Kindle content.

1. Tap the center of a page while you're reading.

2. Tap the Text icon.

3. Tap a font size option to make the text larger or smaller.

4. Tap a Line Spacing option to change the space between lines.

5. Tap a Margins option to change the page margin.

6. Tap a Color Mode to change the color of pages and text.

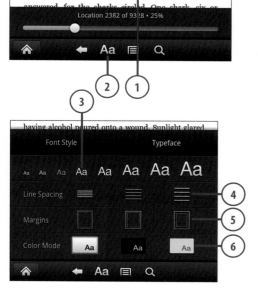

PHIL FELT AS IF HE WERE ON FIRE. THE EQUATORIAL SUN LAY upon the men, scalding their skin. Their upper lips burned and cracked, ballooning so dramatically that they obstructed their nostrils, while their lower lips bulged against their chins. Their bodies were slashed with open cracks that formed under the corrosive onslaught of sun, salt, wind, and fuel residue. Whitecaps slapped into the fissures, a sensation that Louie compared to having alcohol poured onto a wound. Sunlight glared off the ocean, sending barbs of white light into the men's pupils and leaving their heads pounding. The men's feet were cratered with quarter-sized salt sores. The rafts baked along with their occupants, emitting a bitter smell.

The water cans were empty. Desperately thirsty and overheated, the men could do no more than use their hands to bail seawater over themselves. The coolness of the ocean beckoned and couldn't be

Location 2382 of 9318 • 25%

Font Style   Typeface

Line Spacing

Margins

Color Mode

Changing the Typeface

By default, the Kindle Fire displays type using the Georgia typeface. You can choose from a selection of typefaces if Georgia isn't to your liking.

1. Tap the center of a page while you're reading.

2. Tap the Text icon.

3. Tap Typeface.

4. Scroll to the desired typeface.

5. Tap the typeface.

Font Styles and Typeface Are Not Just in Books

You can change font styles and typeface settings in books, newspapers, personal documents, and in magazines. You can change the text size in Silk (the Kindle Fire's web browser) as well, and I'll show you how in Chapter 10, "Browsing the Web with Silk."

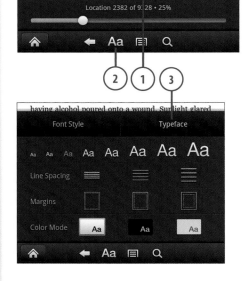

Using Notes

Just like writing in the margins of a physical book, notes are a convenient way of annotating a book. Notes are available in books and in personal documents that are in Mobi format. (Kindle files in Mobi format have either a .mobi or a .prc file extension.)

Adding a Note

You can add a note to any book, whether you own the book or not. Notes that you add to a book are synchronized across all of your Kindle devices and Kindle apps.

1. In an open book, tap and hold to begin selecting a passage to which you'd like to attach a note.

2. If necessary, tap and drag on the left and right of a selection to select more or fewer words.

3. Tap Note.

4. Enter the text for your note using the Kindle keyboard.

5. Tap Save to save the note.

6. To cancel a note, tap away from the Note pop-up.

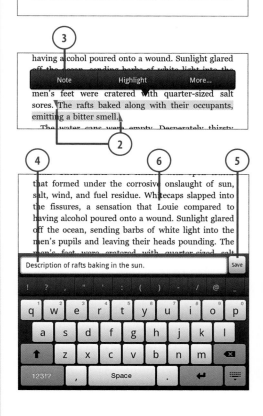

Viewing an Individual Note

Notes appear as highlighted text with a blue note icon. You can view an individual note by tapping it.

1. Tap the blue note icon that marks your note.

2. After reviewing your note, tap Close.

Viewing All Notes

You can view a list of all of your notes, highlights, and bookmarks.

1. Tap the center of a page to access the Options bar.

2. Tap the Menu icon.

3. Scroll up and down to see all of your notes and marks.

4. Tap a note or mark to go to that location in the book.

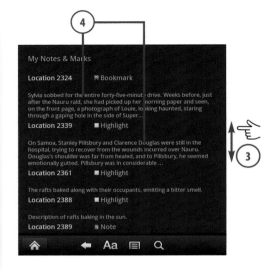

Editing a Note

You can easily edit notes and any edits you make are synchronized across all of your Kindle devices.

1. Tap on the middle of a page in the book that contains the note you want to edit.

2. Tap the Menu icon.

3. Tap and hold the note you want to edit.

4. Tap Edit.

5. Enter the new text for your note.

6. Tap Save to commit your changes to the note. You'll be returned to reading the page where the note is located.

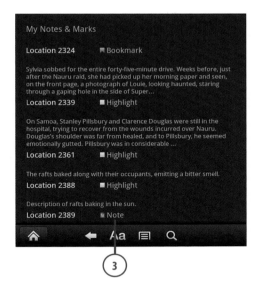

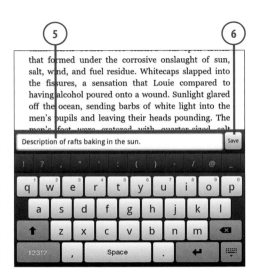

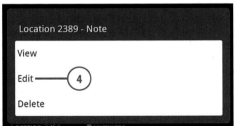

Deleting a Note

When you delete a note, it deletes it across all of your Kindle devices.

1. Tap the middle of a page in the book that contains the note you want to delete.

2. Tap the Menu icon.

3. Tap and hold the note that you want to delete.

4. Tap Delete.

Pʜɪʟ ꜰᴇʟᴛ ᴀs ɪꜰ ʜᴇ ᴡᴇʀᴇ ᴏɴ ꜰɪʀᴇ. ᴛʜᴇ ᴇQᴜᴀᴛᴏʀɪᴀʟ sᴜɴ ʟᴀʏ upon the men, scalding their skin. Their upper lips burned and cracked, ballooning so dramatically that they obstructed their nostrils, while their lower lips bulged against their chins. Their bodies were slashed with open cracks that formed under the corrosive onslaught of sun, salt, wind, and fuel residue. Whitecaps slapped into the fissures, a sensation that Louie compared to having alcohol poured onto a wound. Sunlight glared off the ocean, sending barbs of white light into the men's pupils and leaving their heads pounding. The men's feet were cratered with quarter-sized salt sores. The rafts baked along with their occupants, emitting a bitter smell.

The water cans were empty. Desperately thirsty and overheated, the men could do no more than use their hands to bail seawater over themselves. The coolness of the ocean beckoned and couldn't be answered for the sharks circled. One shark, six or

Location 2382 of 9328 • 25%

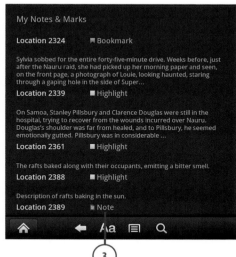

My Notes & Marks

Location 2324   ⚑ Bookmark

Sylvia sobbed for the entire forty-five-minute drive. Weeks before, just after the Nauru raid, she had picked up her morning paper and seen, on the front page, a photograph of Louie, looking haunted, staring through a gaping hole in the side of Super...

Location 2339   ■ Highlight

On Samoa, Stanley Pillsbury and Clarence Douglas were still in the hospital, trying to recover from the wounds incurred over Nauru. Douglas's shoulder was far from healed, and to Pillsbury, he seemed emotionally gutted. Pillsbury was in considerable ...

Location 2361   ■ Highlight

The rafts baked along with their occupants, emitting a bitter smell.

Location 2388   ■ Highlight

Description of rafts baking in the sun.

Location 2389   ▮ Note

Location 2389 - Note

View

Edit

Delete

Working with Highlights

Highlights are a convenient way to mark passages that are important or that you want to review later on. Highlights are available in books and in personal documents that are in Mobi format. You cannot highlight periodicals.

Notes Are Also Highlights

When you add a note to a passage, a highlight is added as well.

Adding a Highlight

Just like highlights in a physical book, a highlighted passage in a Kindle Fire book appears as yellow highlighted words.

1. Tap and hold to begin selecting a passage you'd like to highlight.

2. If necessary, tap and drag on the left and right of a selection to select more or fewer words.

3. Tap Highlight.

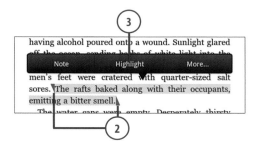

① off the ocean, sending barbs of white light into the men's pupils and leaving their heads pounding. The men's feet er smell. d with quarter-sized salt sores. The r ong with their occupants, emitting a bitter smell.

The water cans were empty. Desperately thirsty and overheated, the men could do no more than use their hands to bail seawater over themselves. The coolness of the ocean beckoned and couldn't be answered, for the sharks circled. One shark, six or eight feet long, stalked the rafts without rest, day and night. The men became especially wary of him, and when he ventured too close, one of them would

③ having alcohol poured onto a wound. Sunlight glared

| Note | Highlight | More... |

men's feet were cratered with quarter-sized salt sores. The rafts baked along with their occupants, emitting a bitter smell.

The water cans were empty. Desperately thirsty

②

Deleting a Highlight

Unlike highlights in a physical book, you can delete a highlight in a Kindle book.

1. Tap on the middle of a page in the book that contains the highlight you want to delete.

2. Tap the Menu icon.

3. Locate the highlight you'd like to delete.

4. Tap and hold the highlight and tap Delete.

No Confirmation for Deleting Highlights

When you delete a highlight, you aren't asked whether you really want to delete it. If you think about it, this isn't really a big deal because you can just highlight a passage again if you accidentally delete it.

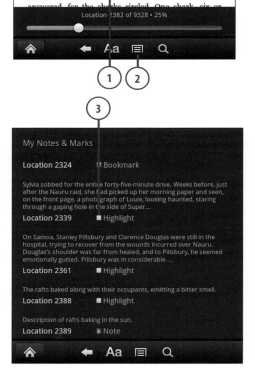

Working with Bookmarks

When you're reading a physical book, a bookmark allows you to mark your place so that you can easily return to it. The Kindle Fire marks your place automatically, but you still may want to add bookmarks on important pages so that you can easily locate them later. Think of these bookmarks as a dog-eared page. In fact, you can bookmark as many pages as you wish in a book.

Bookmarks are available in books and in personal documents that are in Mobi format.

Adding a Bookmark

Adding a bookmark is easy. Bookmarks that you add are synchronized across all of your Kindle devices and applications.

1. Move to the page where you'd like to add your bookmark.

2. Tap the middle of the page to bring up the Options bar and bookmark icon.

3. Tap the bookmark icon to add a bookmark.

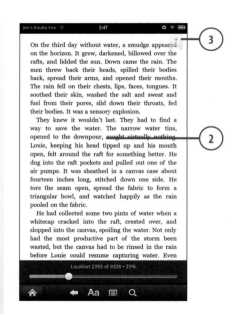

Removing a Bookmark

When you remove a bookmark, it removes it from all Kindle devices and applications.

1. Move to the page that is bookmarked.

2. Tap the blue bookmark icon to remove the bookmark.

Easy Bookmark Removal

Bookmarks can also be deleted from the My Notes and Marks screen. Tap and hold the bookmark and tap Delete.

Moving to a Bookmark

You can easily move directly to a page that you've bookmarked using the My Notes and Marks screen.

1. Tap the center of a page while reading your book.

2. Tap the Menu icon.

3. Scroll to the bookmark.

4. Tap the bookmark to move directly to that bookmark.

Reading Magazines and Newspapers

The Kindle Fire is a wonderful way to read magazines and newspapers. The full-color screen and the touch interface make the experience of reading periodicals much better than on previous Kindles.

Reading a Page View-Enabled Magazine

Many magazines that are available in the Kindle Store are Page View Enabled, which means that they provide two views; Page View and Text View. Page View represents the look of the actual printed magazine. Text View is a view that is better suited to reading because of the focus on text rather than graphics.

Magazines that have Page View are labeled as Magazine - Page View Enabled in the Newsstand store. These magazines open in Page View by default.

1. From Newsstand, tap a magazine that is Page View enabled to open it.

2. Tap the center of a page to display page thumbnails.

3. Tap a page thumbnail to move to that page. The current page is outlined in blue.

4. Use the slider to quickly move to a specific page.

5. Tap the Contents icon to see a list of articles.

Unread and Read Articles

In the list of articles, unread articles are displayed with white text and articles that you've read are displayed in gray text.

6. Tap an article to move directly to the article.

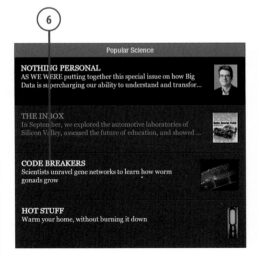

7. Swipe left to move forward one page or swipe right to move back one page. You can also tap the right edge of a page to page forward and the left edge to page backward.

8. Double-tap or reverse pinch to zoom into a page.

9. Slide to move to a particular place on the page.

10. Double-tap or pinch to zoom out.

11. Tap on the center of a page containing text.

12. Tap the Contents icon and tap Text View to switch to Text View.

Reading in Text View

When in Text View, a Page View-enabled magazine is just like a magazine that's not Page View enabled.

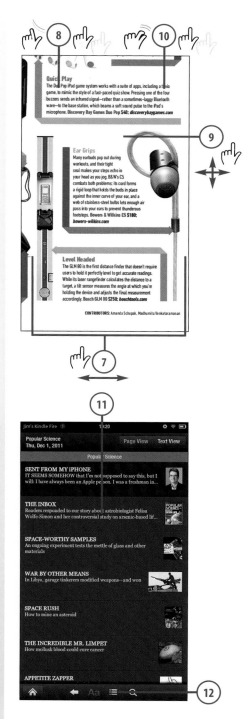

Reading in Text View and Reading Newspapers

Magazines that aren't Page View enabled always display in Text View and do not offer the option of displaying in Page View. The experience of reading a magazine in Text View and reading a newspaper is identical.

1. From the Newsstand, tap a magazine that is not Page View enabled or tap a newspaper.

2. Tap the center of a page to show the Progress and Options bars.

3. Tap the arrows on the Progress bar to move forward and backwards through articles.

4. Tap the Text icon to change text size, typeface, and color options.

5. Tap the Contents icon to display a list of articles and sections.

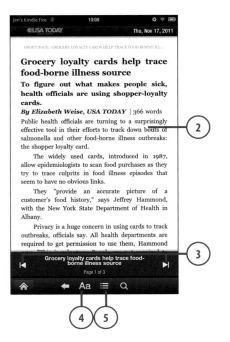

6. Tap an article to go to that article.

7. Swipe left to move forward one page or swipe right to move back one page. You can also tap the right edge of a page to page forward and the left edge to page backward.

Newspaper Sections

Many newspapers have a Sections button in the upper left that makes it easy to quickly move to a specific section.

Managing Personal Documents

In addition to Kindle content from Amazon, your Kindle Fire also directly supports reading of text files and Adobe PDF files. Other file types are supported, but they first have to be converted to a format that the Kindle Fire can handle.

Emailing a Personal Document to Kindle Fire

The easiest way to convert a document for reading on your Kindle Fire is by emailing the document to your kindle.com email address. When you do, the Kindle Personal Document Service converts the document for you and delivers it to your Kindle over the Wi-Fi connection.

1. If you don't already know your kindle.com email address, tap Docs from the Home screen to display it.

2. Create a new email message on your computer addressed to your kindle.com address.

3. Attach the document you want to convert to the email message.

4. Send the email message.

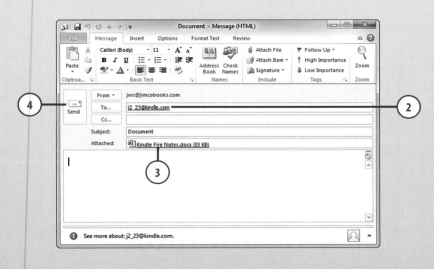

Supported File Types

The Kindle Personal Document Service can convert Microsoft Word documents, Rich Text format, HTML files, compressed documents in Zip or X-Zip format, and Mobi books.

It's Not All Good

Only email addresses that are on your Approved Personal Document E-Mail List can successfully send documents to your Kindle email address. After all, you don't want strangers sending documents to your Kindle and incurring costs for conversion, do you? You can add emails to your list from the Manage Your Kindle page, and you can read more information on doing that in Chapter 4.

Sideloading Personal Documents

You can sideload personal documents, as described earlier in this chapter, as long as they are in a format that the Kindle Fire supports natively. You should convert files that are not natively supported by the Kindle Fire using the Kindle Personal Document Service or a tool such as Calibre. (Calibre is discussed in detail in Chapter 5.)

1. Connect your Kindle Fire to your computer using a micro-USB cable.

2. Wait until your Kindle Fire notifies you that you can transfer files to it.

You can now transfer files from your computer to Kindle.

When you are done, press the disconnect button at the bottom of the screen or eject your Kindle from your computer, and then disconnect the USB cable.

3. Open your Kindle Fire on your computer and locate the Documents folder.

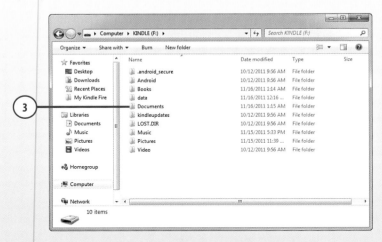

4. Copy your personal document to the Documents folder.

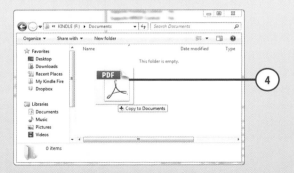

5. Disconnect your Kindle Fire from your computer.

Changing Personal Document Titles and Authors

The title and author of your personal documents might not be what you want them to be. You can easily edit them using Calibre. Read more about Calibre in Chapter 5.

Reading Personal Documents

Your experience in reading personal documents differs depending on what type of file the document is. Personal documents in Mobi eBook format have all of the features you're used to from Kindle books, but other formats offer only a basic reading experience.

Deleting Personal Documents

You can easily delete personal documents from your Kindle Fire using the Docs screen.

1. From the Docs screen, tap and hold on the personal document you want to delete.

2. Tap Delete.

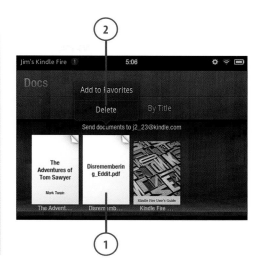

Searching Content

Your Kindle Fire automatically maintains a searchable index of all the content in your libraries. You can also search in Wikipedia or Google.

Searching the Current Item

You can search for one or more words in an item that you're reading.

1. While reading the item you want to search, tap the middle of a page to access the Options bar.

2. Tap the Search icon.

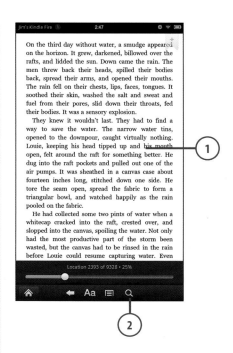

3. Enter your search words in the Search box.

4. Tap Go.

5. Wait for the progress bar while the search completes.

6. Scroll to locate a specific search result.

7. Tap to move to the search result in the text.

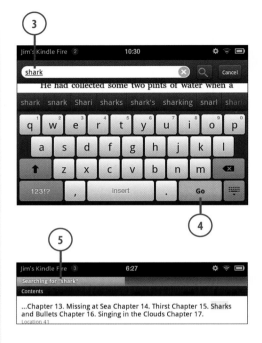

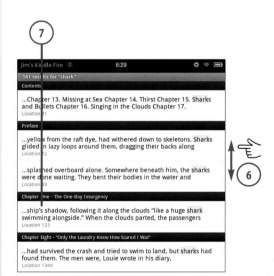

Searching Wikipedia or Google from Books

You can search Google or Wikipedia for words that you select in books. If you select more than two words, these options won't be available.

1. Select one or two words for which you'd like to search.

2. Tap More.

3. Tap Search Wikipedia to search for the selected word(s) in Wikipedia.

4. Tap Search Google to search for the selected word(s) in Google.

5. After you've finished reading the search results, tap the Menu icon.

6. Tap Back to Reading to go back to your book.

Going Back

The Back icon can take you back to reading as well, but if you've clicked a link in the search results, the Back icon takes you back to the page you were viewing before you clicked the link. If you want to return to reading in one step, use the Back to Reading menu item.

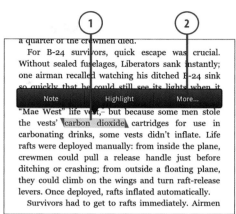

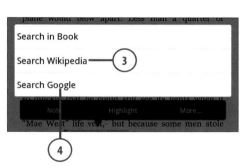

Searching Wikipedia or Google from Periodicals and Personal Document

Searching Wikipedia or Google from periodicals and personal documents is performed a little differently than from books.

1. Select one or two words for which you'd like to search.

2. Tap Wikipedia to search for the selected word(s) in Wikipedia.

3. Tap Google to search for the selected word(s) in Google.

4. When finished reading search results, tap the Menu icon.

5. Tap Back to Reading.

Personal Documents and Books

Remember that personal documents that are in Mobi format are treated as books and not personal documents. Therefore, search in Mobi files works just as it does with books.

WILD THINGS · WILD THINGS

Wild Things
LIFE AS WE KNOW IT

PAUL MAREK / UNIVERSITY OF ARIZONA (CURRENT BIOLOGY, SEP. 27, 2011)

BY T.A. FRAIL, JOSEPH STROMBERG, ABIGAIL TUCKER, ERIN WAYMAN AND

Search   Wikipedia   Google

WARNING LIGHT

Nocturnal millipedes in the genus Motyxia glow in the dark (above). But why? Being blind, they're not lighting up to impress one another. Scientists

Manage Content   Manage Devices

Your Account > **Manage Your Kindle**   Kindle Help ⊡

Your Kindle Library   **Your Kindle Library**

All Items   View: [Books ▾]   OR   Search your library   (GO)
Books
Newspapers   Showing 1 - 15 of 198 items
Magazines
Blogs   Title   Author   Date ▾
Personal Documents   ⊕ Forty-Four (44)   Sinclair, Jools   November 22, 2011   [Actions... ▾]
Audible Audiobooks   ⊕ Unbroken: A World War II Story of Hillenbrand, Laura   October 26, 2011   [Actions... ▾]
Active Content   Survival, Resilience, and Redemption
Pending Deliveries   [1]   ⊕ Mixing Secrets   Senior, Mike   October 15, 2011   [Actions... ▾]
                               ⊕ How to Measure Anything: Finding the
Your Kindle Account   Value of Intangibles in Business Hubbard, Douglas W.   September 13, 2011   [Actions... ▾]

Register a Kindle   ⊕ The Friend Request   Ford, Alex   July 13, 2011   [Actions... ▾]
Manage Your Devices ●   ⊕ Einstein's Refrigerator: And Other
Subscription Settings   Stories from the Flip Side of History Silverman, Steve   July 13, 2011   [Actions... ▾]
Kindle Payment Settings   ⊕ Through the Fire   Grady, Shawn   July 7, 2011   [Actions... ▾]
Personal Document Settings   ⊕ Back on Murder (Roland March
Country Settings   Mysteries)   Bertrand, J. Mark   July 7, 2011   [Actions... ▾]
                                                                  Gibson, William, Ono,
Other Digital Content   ⊕ 2:46: Aftershocks: Stories from the Yoko, Eisler, Barry,
                                  Japan Earthquake   Adelstein, Jake, The   June 1, 2011   [Actions... ▾]
Manage Your MP3s   quakebook community
Manage Your Videos   ⊕ No Good Deed: Book One of the Mark
Manage Your Apps   Taylor Series (A Psychological Thriller) McDonald, M.P.   June 1, 2011   [Actions... ▾]
                               ⊕ Blood of My Brother   Lepore, James   June 1, 2011   [Actions... ▾]

                               « Previous | Page: 1 2 3 ... | Next »

Manage MP3s   Manage Your
and More   Account

In this chapter, you'll learn how you can use Amazon's Manage Your Kindle page to keep track of your books, your subscriptions, and manage your payment and device information.

→ Working with Books and Docs

→ Managing Subscriptions

→ Updating Kindle Payment Information

→ Managing Your Kindle Devices

Using Amazon's Manage Your Kindle Page

Amazon's Manage Your Kindle page is a one-stop location for managing your Kindle content and your Kindle devices. If you have multiple Kindle devices, the Manage Your Kindle page is even more useful.

You can use the Manage Your Kindle page to send books from your Kindle library to any of your Kindle devices. You can also use it to see the periodicals you subscribe to, and you can manage those subscriptions as well. There are also links to manage your method of payment to Amazon so that you can ensure that items you purchase on your Kindle Fire get charged to the right credit card. Finally, you can register and deregister Kindles and rename your Kindle from the Manage Your Kindle page.

Working with Books and Docs

You can view all of the books and docs in your library using Manage Your Kindle. You can also transfer them to your Kindle. Books are eBooks that you've purchased from Amazon's Kindle store. Your docs can also be eBooks, but ones that you purchased from a third-party or obtained from another source other than Amazon. Docs that you see listed in Manage Your Kindle have been emailed to your kindle.com email address for document conversion. Manage Your Kindle won't list docs that you sideload to your Kindle Fire using the micro-USB cable.

What's Up with Docs?

When I talk about "docs," I'm talking about Kindle Personal Documents. I use the term "docs" because the Kindle Fire uses the Docs screen for your Personal Documents.

Docs are covered in detail in the Managing Personal Documents section in Chapter 3, "Reading on the Kindle Fire."

Accessing Manage Your Kindle

Manage Your Kindle is a web page that you access using the Web browser on your computer or using Silk on your Kindle Fire.

1. Open your web browser.

2. Browse to www.amazon.com/manageyourkindle.

3. Log in using your email address and Amazon password if prompted.

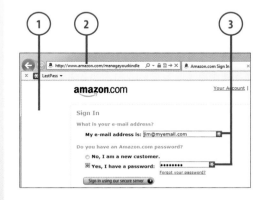

Viewing Books and Docs

Manage Your Kindle's default view shows you your Kindle books, but you can view other content types as well. I talk about handling newspapers and magazines in the next section. This section covers just books and docs.

From the Manage Your Kindle page, you can select the type of content you want to view using the View dropdown. Content can be sorted by title, author, or by date by clicking on one of the column headers. The first click of a column header sorts in ascending order, and if you click the same column header again, that column will sort in descending order.

If you want to see details on an item, click the plus sign next to the item title. If you have a lot of content and you want to search for a particular item, enter a search term and click Go.

Select type of content you want to see from the View drop-down.　　**Search for an item by entering a search item.**　　**Click a column header to order the list by title, author, or date.**

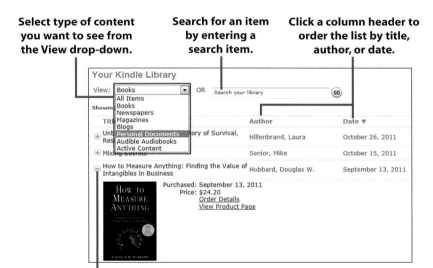

View item details by clicking the plus sign next to the title.

Why Use Manage Your Kindle?

A lot of the functionality in Manage Your Kindle is also available on your Kindle Fire. However, if you have multiple Kindles, Manage Your Kindle is a great way to manage content on all of them. It's also convenient to use Manage Your Kindle when someone else in the family is using your Kindle Fire, something that's likely to happen.

Sending Books and Docs to Your Kindle

You can send books and docs to a Kindle device. Books can also be sent to the Kindle app running on your computer or a mobile device. Content is delivered to your Kindle within a minute, assuming you are connected to Wi-Fi.

Kindle Apps

When I mention Kindle apps in this chapter, I'm not talking about apps installed on your Kindle Fire. I'm talking about the Kindle app that you can use on a computer, iPad, or your mobile phone.

1. Locate the book or doc that you want to send to your Kindle.

2. Point to the Actions drop-down.

3. Click on Deliver to My.

4. Select the device from the drop-down. If the doc you are sending to your Kindle isn't in a format supported by a particular device, that device is not available in the drop-down.

5. Click Deliver.

Sending Docs

Docs can only be sent to Kindle devices. You cannot send them to a computer or mobile device running the Kindle app.

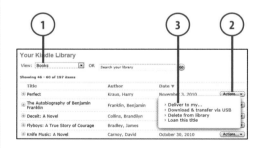

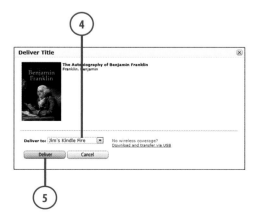

Downloading Books to a Computer

You can download books to your computer. (This option is not available for docs.) After you download a book, you need to sideload it to your Kindle using the micro-USB cable.

1. Point to the Actions drop-down.

2. Click Download & Transfer via USB.

3. Select the Kindle to which you plan to transfer the book.

4. Click Download.

5. Save the book using your browser's download option.

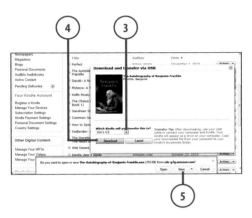

Deleting Books and Docs

You can delete books and docs from your library. Be very careful here because doing so removes the item permanently. If you delete a book that you purchased from Amazon, you have to buy it again if you want to read it.

1. Point to the Actions drop-down.

2. Click Delete from Library.

3. Click Yes to confirm that you want to delete the book from your library.

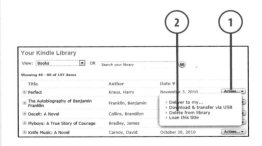

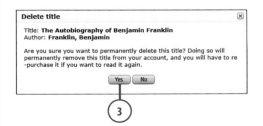

Changing Your Kindle Email Address for Docs

Your Kindle email address is used to send docs directly to your Kindle. You can change the Kindle email address for your Kindle on the Manage Your Kindle page.

1. Click Personal Document Settings.

2. Click Edit next to the Kindle email address you want to change.

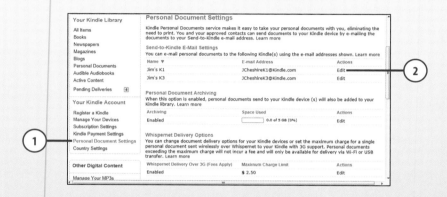

3. Enter the new email address.

4. Click Update.

Creative Addresses

I admit that I tend to be boring with my email addresses, but you don't have to be. You can choose any email name you want. If the email address you specify has already been used (including by you for another one of your Kindles), Amazon informs you that you need to choose a different address.

Limiting Doc Conversion Charges

There is no charge for the delivery of converted docs to the Kindle Fire because it's Wi-Fi only. However, if you have a 3G Kindle and your personal document is delivered over the 3G connection, Amazon charges you 15 cents per megabyte in the United States and 99 cents per megabyte outside of the United States.

You can place a limit on your doc conversion charges for each document so that any delivery that would cost you more than a certain amount is not sent over 3G. You can also disable the personal document delivery service.

1. From Personal Document Settings (see "Changing Your Kindle Email Address for Docs" earlier in this chapter), click Edit in the Whispernet Delivery Options section.

2. Enter a maximum per document delivery charge amount.

3. Click Update.

Disabling Delivery over Whispernet

You can disable delivery over Whispernet altogether by unchecking the Enable Delivery to my Kindle over Whispernet checkbox.

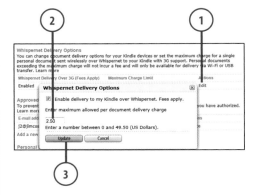

Adding an Approved Email for Docs

Amazon only converts and delivers docs emailed to your Kindle email address if the sending email is on your approved email list. You can add an approved email address using Personal Document Settings.

1. From Personal Document Settings (see "Changing Your Kindle Email Address for Docs" earlier in this chapter), click Add a New Approved E-mail Address in the Approved Personal Document E-mail List section.

2. Enter the email address you want to approve. You can also enter a partial email address such as "yourcompany.com" in order to allow all senders from that particular domain.

3. Click Add Address.

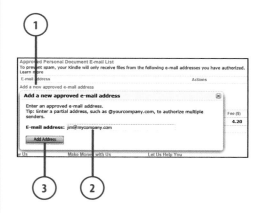

Deleting an Approved Email Address

You can delete an approved email address by clicking Delete next to the email address, as shown here.

List of authorized email addresses.

Click to remove an authorized email address.

Disabling Doc Archiving

By default, docs that are sent to your Kindle are also saved in your Kindle library. Amazon gives you 5GB of space for personal doc archiving, so you might not want to save all of your personal docs in your Kindle library. You can disable the archiving of personal docs.

1. From Personal Document Settings, click Edit in the Personal Document Archiving section.

2. Uncheck the box to disable archiving.

3. Click Update.

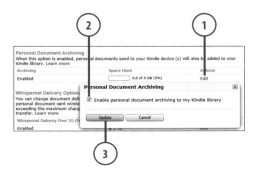

Managing Subscriptions

You can also manage your subscriptions from the Manage Your Kindle page. You can choose which device gets your subscription automatically, send past issues to your Kindle Fire, or download past issues so that you can sideload them to your Kindle Fire. Finally, you can cancel your subscription altogether.

Changing Where a Subscription Is Delivered

You choose which device receives the automatic delivery of subscription content when you first subscribe. You can change that choice from Manage Your Kindle. This option is only available if you have multiple Kindle devices registered.

1. Click Subscription Settings.

2. Click Edit for the subscription you want to change.

3. Select a device to which new editions should be delivered.

4. Click Update.

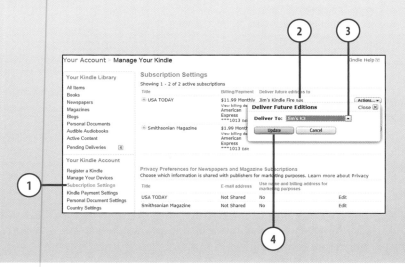

Canceling a Subscription

If you want to cancel a subscription, you can do it from Manage Your Kindle.

1. From Subscription Settings, click Actions for the subscription you'd like to cancel.

2. Click Cancel Subscription.

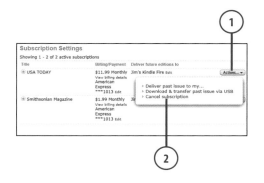

3. Select one or more reasons for canceling.

4. Enter a comment if you select Other.

5. Click Cancel Subscription.

Access to Past Issues for Canceled Subscriptions

If you cancel a subscription, any issues that have been down-loaded to your Kindle remain in your library. However, you won't be able to download any past issues.

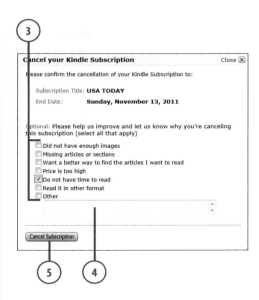

Reactivating a Canceled Subscription

Amazon maintains a list of all of your inactive subscriptions. You can use this list to easily reactivate a canceled subscription.

1. From Subscription Settings, click View Inactive Subscriptions.

2. Click Actions for the subscription you want to reactivate.

3. Click Reactivate Subscription.

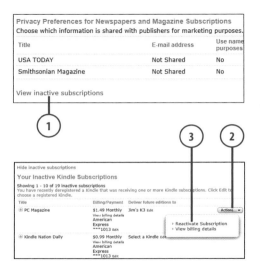

4. Click Reactivate Subscription in the confirmation dialog.

Why Is the Actions Button Missing?

If you have deregistered the Kindle to which an inactive subscription was being delivered, the Actions button is missing. Before you can reactivate the subscription, you first need to select a Kindle to which the subscription should be delivered.

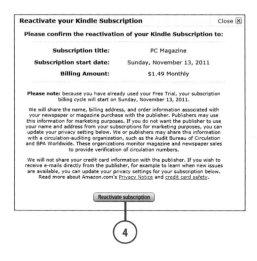

Changing Subscription Privacy Settings

Amazon does not share your email address with content providers unless you explicitly give permission to do so. You can do that using subscription privacy settings.

1. From Subscription Settings, locate Privacy Preferences for Newspapers and Magazine Subscriptions.

2. Click Edit for the subscription you'd like to modify.

3. Check the box(es) for the information you'd like to share with the content provider.

4. If you'd like for your settings to be the default for future subscriptions, check the appropriate box.

5. Click Update.

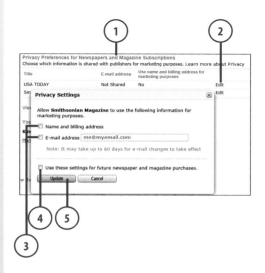

Updating Kindle Payment Information

You can change the credit card that Amazon uses for purchases and for current subscriptions.

Changing Amazon Purchases Credit Card

When you buy Kindle books, MP3s, and rent or purchase Amazon videos, the credit card used for 1-Click purchases at Amazon.com is billed automatically. You can change this credit card information, add a new credit card, or choose a different credit card using Manage Your Kindle.

Multiple Credit Cards

Amazon can store several credit cards for your account, and you can choose which one is used for your 1-Click purchases on the Manage Your Kindle page. Keep in mind that changing your credit card will not change the credit card used for your subscriptions. Those have to be changed separately.

---

1. Click Kindle Payment Settings.

2. Click Edit.

3. Enter your new credit card information or select a different card.

4. Click Continue.

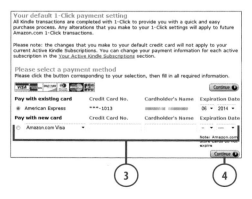

Changing Current Subscriptions Credit Card

Changing your 1-Click credit card does not change the card used for billing of current subscriptions. You must individually update payment options for current subscriptions .

1. From Kindle Payment Settings, click Edit Payment for the subscription you'd like to change.

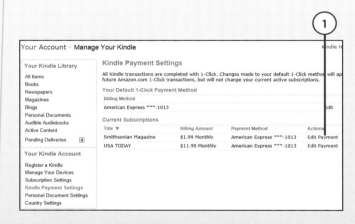

2. Enter the new credit card information.

3. Click Continue.

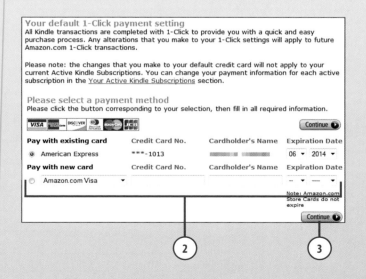

Managing Your Kindle Devices

You can add multiple Kindles to your account, and all of them will be listed in Manage Your Kindle. Having two Kindles registered to the same account is useful if you and another family member have the same tastes in books. If you buy a book on one Kindle, you can read it on the other Kindle at the same time without having to buy it again.

All of your Kindle devices (including the Kindle app installed on your computer or other devices) will be listed on the Manage Your Kindle page. You can deregister a Kindle or change your Kindle's name.

It's Not All Good

Registering a Kindle at Amazon.com

You can also register a new Kindle from the Manage Your Kindle page, but to do so, you need the serial number of the Kindle you're registering. You can't find the serial number for a Kindle Fire without first starting the device and going through the initial setup, part of which is registering the device with Amazon. Therefore, it doesn't make sense to use the Manage Your Kindle page to register a Kindle Fire.

Deregistering a Kindle

If you decided to give away or sell your Kindle, you should deregister it first.

1. From Manage Your Devices, locate the Kindle you want to deregister.

2. Click Deregister.

3. Click the Deregister button.

Renaming Your Kindle

You can change the name of your Kindle device from Manage Your Kindle.

1. From Manage Your Devices, locate the Kindle whose name you want to change.

2. Click Edit next to the existing name.

3. Enter a new name for your Kindle.

4. Click Update.

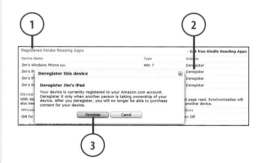

Deregistering a Kindle App

You can also deregister a Kindle app on your computer, iPad, or mobile device.

1. From Manage Your Devices, locate the Registered Kindle Reading Apps section.

2. Click Deregister for the app you want to deregister.

3. Click the Deregister button.

Why Deregister an App?

If you are going to lend your computer or device to a friend, or if you are giving away your computer or device, you should first deregister the Kindle app. That way, no purchases can be made against your account without your knowledge.

Turning Whispersync Off

Whispersync keeps all of your devices and Kindle apps synchronized. It synchronizes your reading position, notes, highlights, and more. You normally want to keep Whispersync turned on, but if multiple people in your home are reading Kindles registered to the same account and those people are also reading the same book, Whispersync should be disabled.

1. In Manage Your Devices, locate the Device Synchronization section.

2. Click Turn Off to turn off Whispersync. This change takes effect immediately.

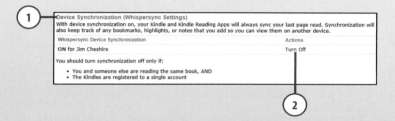

Turning Whispersync Back On

When you click Turn Off, the link changes to Turn On. You can turn Whispersync back on by clicking Turn On.

Edit Author,
Title, and
Cover

Convert and
Transfer to your
Kindle Fire

Manage
eBooks on
Your Computer

In this chapter, you learn how you can use a free tool called Calibre to manage eBooks that you download from sources other than Amazon.

→ Getting Started with Calibre

→ Adding Content to Calibre

→ Editing Book Information

→ Transferring eBooks to the Kindle Fire

Managing Content with Calibre

Amazon's Kindle Store offers millions of books that you can read on your Kindle Fire, but Amazon certainly doesn't have a corner on the eBook market. Sites such as www.feedbooks.com and www.baen.com have plenty of eBooks that you can read on your Kindle.

Buying eBooks from Amazon gives you the benefit of having those eBooks stored in the cloud on Amazon's servers, an advantage that you don't get with third-party eBooks vendors. However, by using a tool like Calibre, you can easily manage your third-party eBooks.

Calibre Updates

Calibre is updated often, and it's possible that by the time you read this chapter, the steps may have changed slightly. I wrote this chapter based on version 0.8.29 of Calibre.

Getting Started with Calibre

Calibre is available from calibre-ebook.com. Because Calibre needs to be installed on your computer, you need to access that URL from your computer and not your Kindle Fire. (You can download Calibre in both Windows and Mac versions.)

Welcome Wizard

After you've downloaded and installed Calibre, you can launch it and walk through the Welcome Wizard.

1. Choose your language.

2. Choose a folder for your Calibre library. If you already have eBooks on your computer that you want Calibre to manage, choose the folder that contains them. Otherwise, you can accept the default.

Creating a Calibre Library

If you don't already have a Calibre library, make sure you point Calibre to an empty directory where it creates a new library for you. It doesn't matter where you create this folder. It's purely up to you.

3. Click Next.

4. Select Amazon as the manufacturer and Kindle Fire as the device.

5. Click Next.

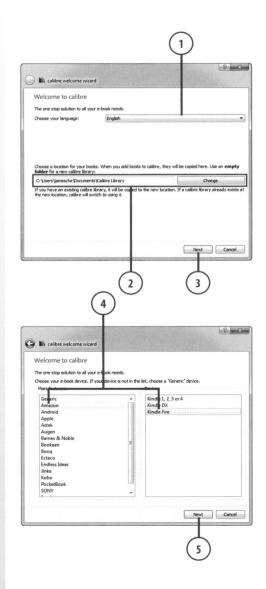

6. Click Finish to start using Calibre.

Demo videos
Videos demonstrating the various features of calibre are available online.
User Manual
A User Manual is also available online.

6

Finish   Cancel

Adding Content to Calibre

If you already have eBooks in the folder you chose in the Welcome Wizard, Calibre should already be populated with your eBooks. Otherwise, you need to import any existing eBooks into Calibre.

>>> Go Further

EBOOK FORMATS

eBooks come in many different formats. The most popular eBook format is called EPUB, and it's the format that libraries have used for the past few years. The Kindle is the only common eBook reader that does not support EPUB format. Instead, the Kindle supports the MOBI format.

eBooks that you purchase from the Kindle store are actually in AZW format. The AZW format is a derivative of MOBI. Amazon modified the format slightly in order to accommodate its serial number format and to add digital rights management (DRM) so that you can't buy a book once and give it to a million Internet users.

As long as you have eBooks that don't have DRM embedded in them, you can usually convert them to MOBI format for your Kindle Fire. Unfortunately, it's not a simple task to tell if a book is protected with DRM. The easiest way is to try to use the book with Calibre. It will complain if the book is protected with DRM.

Importing Books

You can import eBooks in any format into your Calibre library. If an eBook is in a format that your Kindle Fire doesn't recognize, Calibre can convert it for you.

1. Click Add Books.

2. Browse to the folder on your computer that contains your eBooks.

3. Select one or more eBooks to add to your Calibre library.

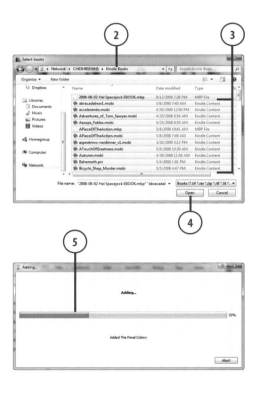

4. Click the Open button to import the selected books into your library.

5. Wait until Calibre finishes importing your eBooks.

6. If Calibre notifies you that it found duplicates, click No so that they won't be imported.

Adding New Books

If you download new eBooks after you've built your Calibre library, you need to add them to Calibre using the Add Books button.

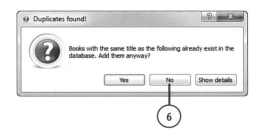

Searching for New eBooks

Calibre has an integrated search engine that makes it easy to locate new eBooks. Calibre's search engine searches eBook stores on the Internet for the search term you enter, and many of these eBook stores sell eBooks that are compatible with your Kindle Fire.

Calibre searches for either authors or titles. In other words, you can't enter "boats" to find books about boats. Instead, you'll find books with "boats" in the title or books written by Mr. or Mrs. Boats.

1. Click Get Books.

2. Click OK in the information dialog.

3. Enter your search query. Calibre searches using only the title and author.

Choosing Book Stores

You can uncheck any book stores that you don't want Calibre to search. As you get more accustomed to the results from certain stores, you'll likely find some that you don't want to search.

4. Click Search.

5. Double-click on a search result to view details in your web browser or to purchase the eBook.

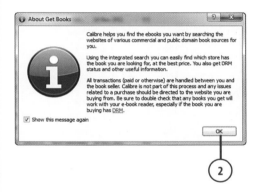

Pay Attention to DRM

Pay special attention to the DRM status of eBooks. If you see a red lock next to a search result, it means that the eBook is protected with DRM and can only be read on certain devices. Your Kindle Fire supports only Amazon Kindle DRM. If a book is DRM protected, and it isn't from the Amazon Kindle Store, it won't open on your Kindle.

It's Not All Good

Use Caution When Searching

Some eBooks that turn up in search results might be copyrighted books that are being offered illegally. It's not a bad idea to only search for eBooks from sources that you know are legitimate. For example, if a site is offering an eBook for free and that same eBook is $10 everywhere else, that's a good sign that something's not right and you might want to avoid that site.

Editing Book Information

Some of your eBooks might not display the correct author or title. The most common cause of this for Kindle users relates to personal docs emailed to your Kindle email address. When Amazon converts these documents, it uses the sending email for the author name. It's easy to use Calibre to edit the author, title, and other information about an eBook.

Downloading Metadata

Calibre can locate information about a particular eBook using well-known book sources such as Amazon and Google.

1. Select the book you want to edit.

2. Click Edit Metadata.

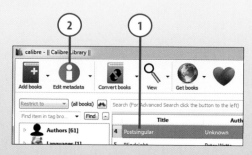

3. Click Download Metadata.

4. Click on the title that matches your search.

5. Click Next.

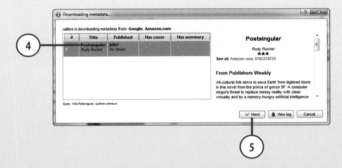

6. Click on a cover picture for your book. Not all results include a book cover.

7. Click OK.

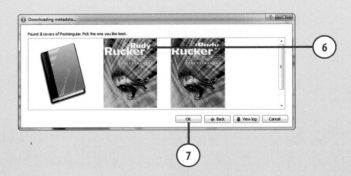

8. Click OK to add the new metadata to your eBook.

⑧

Better Metadata Searching

If you don't find a result when downloading metadata, try adding an ISBN number (you can get it by searching the Books section at Amazon) to the IDs textbox and then clicking Download Metadata.

>>> Go Further

FINDING COVERS

I have to admit that I'm a little bit obsessed about having covers for all of my eBooks. I'm even more obsessed with it now that I have a Kindle Fire with a beautiful color screen.

Calibre can usually locate a cover for your eBooks, but if it can't, an Internet search will usually turn up a cover, very often at Amazon.com. Try searching for the book title in quotes (for example, "The Adventures of Tom Sawyer") and if that doesn't turn up anything, try removing the quotes and adding the author's name. You can increase your chances for success by using the image search available in Bing and Google.

Manually Editing Metadata

If Calibre can't find your eBook when you try to download metadata, you can edit the metadata manually.

1. Enter the new metadata in the Edit Metadata dialog.

2. If you need to add a cover, click Download Cover.

3. Select a cover if one is available.

4. Click OK to add the cover.

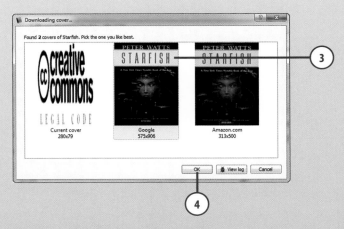

5. Click OK to add the new metadata.

Transferring eBooks to the Kindle Fire

Calibre can sideload books to your Kindle Fire, and if the book requires conversion to Kindle format, Calibre can take care of that as well. In fact, using Calibre to sideload books is preferable because you can use a special technique to make sure that sideloaded books show up in your Books library instead of the Docs library on your Kindle Fire.

The best way to transfer eBooks to your Kindle Fire is a three-step process; convert the eBook to EPUB format, delete all formats except the EPUB format, and auto-convert and transfer the EPUB format to your Kindle Fire.

Add a Cover Before Transferring

Before you use this technique to sideload an eBook to your Kindle Fire, you should add a cover to the eBook's metadata. The technique I show you also transfers the cover art to your Kindle Fire.

Converting to EPUB Format

This step is not necessary if your eBook is already in EPUB format. However, if your book is in any other format, you should convert the eBook to EPUB format before transferring it to your Kindle Fire. The reason you do this is because when Calibre converts an EPUB eBook to a Mobi eBook for your Kindle Fire, it creates a Mobi book that shows up correctly in your Books library.

1. Select the book you want to convert.

2. Click Convert Books.

3. Change the Output Format to EPUB.

4. Check Use Cover from Source File.

5. Click OK.

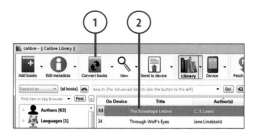

Deleting Non-EPUB Formats

When you transfer the eBook to your Kindle Fire, you should transfer the EPUB format and let Calibre convert it automatically. Therefore, you only need to keep the EPUB format in your Calibre library. This ensures that when you transfer the eBook to your Kindle Fire, it uses the EPUB format and auto-converts it.

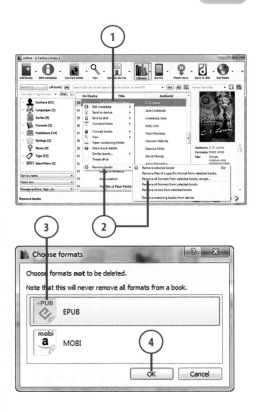

1. Right-click the book you just converted.

2. Point to Remove Books and click on Remove All Formats from Selected Books, Except.

3. Select the EPUB format. This is the format that you want to keep.

4. Click OK.

Transferring the eBook to Your Kindle Fire

Now that you have an EPUB copy of your eBook in your Calibre library, you can transfer the eBook to your Kindle Fire. When you do, Calibre automatically converts the EPUB format to a format that is compatible with your Kindle Fire.

Before you complete these steps, make sure that your Kindle Fire is connected to your computer and that it says that you can transfer files from your computer to your Kindle Fire.

1. Select the eBook that you want to transfer.

2. Click Send to Device.

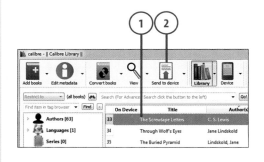

3. Click Yes when asked if you want to convert the eBook.

4. Wait until Calibre shows that the eBook is on your device.

Finding the Sideloaded Book

You can find the book that you sideloaded to your Kindle Fire in your Books library. Tap Books on the Home screen and your new book should appear, complete with any cover art that you added.

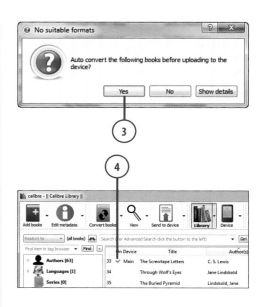

Emailing eBooks to Your Kindle Fire

If you configured email when you set up Calibre, you can have Calibre email eBooks to your Kindle account. The eBook must already be in Microsoft Word, Rich Text, HTML, text, or Mobi format.

1. Right-click on the book that you want to email to your Kindle email address.

2. Point to Connect/Share.

3. Select Setup Email Based Sharing of Books.

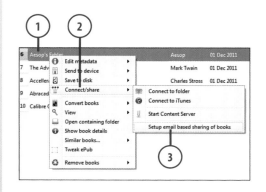

4. Click Add Email.

5. Enter your Kindle email address. (Tap Docs on your Kindle Fire to find your Kindle email address if you're not sure.)

6. Double-click on the formats and delete all of them except for MOBI.

7. Enter your email address (your regular email, not your Kindle email address) in the Send Email From box.

8. Click Use Gmail and enter your Gmail information if you want to use a Gmail account to send the email.

9. Click Use Hotmail and enter your Hotmail information if you want to use a Hotmail account to send the email.

10. If you don't want to use Hotmail or Gmail, enter your email server information to send the email. (If you don't know the email server information, check with your Internet Service Provider.)

11. Click Test Email to test your email settings.

12. Click Apply.

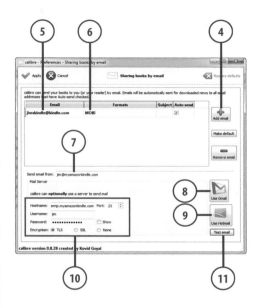

Use an Approved Email

The email address that you configure in Calibre needs to be an email that is on your approved email list for sending docs to your Kindle Fire. For details on adding an email to your approved email list, see "Adding an Approved Email for Docs" in Chapter 4.

Use
Playlists

View Your Cloud
and Device Music

Browse
Music

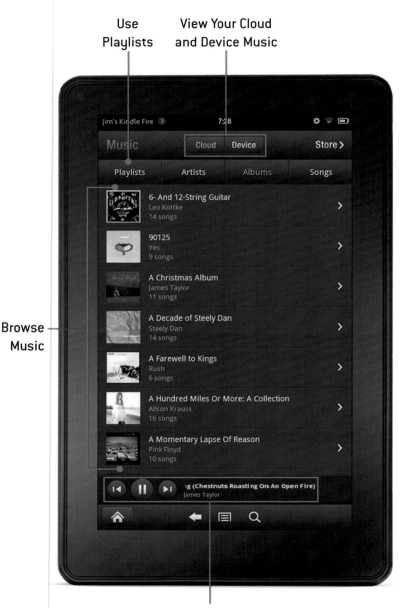

Jim's Kindle Fire 3   7:28   ⚙ 🔆 ▭

Music   Cloud   Device   Store ›

Playlists   Artists   Albums   Songs

6- And 12-String Guitar
Leo Kottke
14 songs   ›

90125
Yes
9 songs   ›

A Christmas Album
James Taylor
11 songs   ›

A Decade of Steely Dan
Steely Dan
14 songs   ›

A Farewell to Kings
Rush
6 songs   ›

A Hundred Miles Or More: A Collection
Alison Krauss
16 songs   ›

A Momentary Lapse Of Reason
Pink Floyd
10 songs   ›

⏮ ⏸ ⏭   g (Chestnuts Roasting On An Open Fire)
                James Taylor

⌂   ⬅ ☰ 🔍

Play Music

In this chapter, you learn how to access and listen to music on your Kindle Fire.

- → Browsing and Downloading Your Music
- → Searching for Music
- → Playing Music
- → Using the Now Playing Queue
- → Managing Playlists
- → Buying New Music
- → Sideloading Music

Accessing and Listening to Music

The Kindle Fire is arguably the best way to play music that you have in the cloud on Amazon's Cloud Drive. Because it has only a bit more than 6GB of user-accessible memory, you likely can't carry all of your music on it when you're offline, but you can make playlists and easily download some of your music to enjoy when you're away from a Wi-Fi connection.

In addition to playing music, you can also browse Amazon's extensive library of MP3s to add to your music collection.

Browsing and Downloading Your Music

Your Kindle Fire integrates directly into your Cloud Drive and provides a first-class interface into browsing and listening to your music. As soon as you start your Kindle Fire for the first time (after you've signed into your Amazon account on the device), it begins indexing the music on your Cloud Drive.

This chapter deals primarily with music in the cloud because that's likely the way you'll listen to music on your Kindle Fire. However, all of the information presented is applicable to interacting with music that is stored on your device.

Add Music to Your Cloud Drive

If you haven't added any music to your Cloud Drive, see Chapter 2, "Amazon's Cloud Services," for information on how you can do that now.

Browsing Artists

Your Kindle Fire can provide you with a list of all artists in your music collection in alphabetical order.

1. From the Home screen, tap Music.

2. Tap Cloud to view your Cloud Drive.

3. Tap Artists to display artists in your collection.

4. Scroll up and down to view artists.

5. Tap an artist to see a list of albums in your collection by the artist.

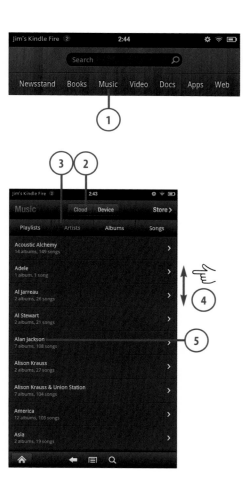

6. Tap Songs to see a list of all songs by the artist.

7. Tap Shop This Artist to open the Amazon Music Store where you can buy songs and albums by the artist you are viewing.

8. Tap Download to download all songs by the artist that you have stored in your Cloud Drive to your device.

9. Tap an album to see details on the album.

10. Tap Download to download the album to your device.

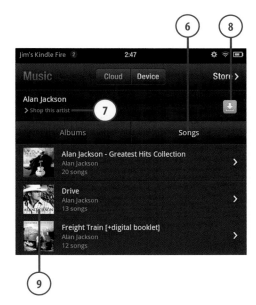

Faster Way to Download an Album

When you are viewing a list of albums from an artist, you can tap and hold an album and then tap Download Album to download it.

11. Tap Music to quickly go back to a list of artists in order to choose a new artist.

Scrolling Quickly in Music

It's not uncommon to have a large number of artists, albums, or songs in your music collection. To make it faster to find a particular item, you can quickly scroll to items that begin with a particular letter of the alphabet.

This technique works in all lists in your Music library.

1. From a list of music items, tap and drag to begin scrolling.

2. As soon as the scroll handle appears, immediately tap and hold it.

3. Drag the scroll handle up and down to quickly browse by letter.

4. Release the scroll handle when the desired letter appears on the screen to jump to items that begin with that letter.

Quick Scroll

Quick scroll is available in most screens while browsing your music collection.

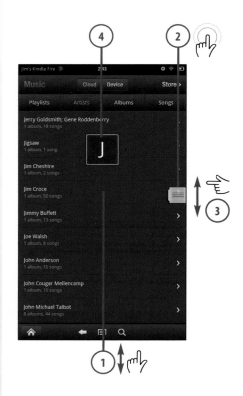

Browsing Albums

You can also view a list of all albums in your collection in alphabetical order.

1. From your Music library, tap Albums to see a list of albums.

2. Scroll to locate the album you want to view or play.

3. Tap the album to see details.

Browsing Songs

You can use this same technique to browse songs on your Cloud Drive.

Monitoring Downloads

Tracks that are being downloaded are added to a list of downloads. You can view the currently downloading track along with completed downloads.

1. From any screen in your Music library, tap the Menu icon.

2. Tap Downloads.

3. Tap the Pause icon to pause the current download.

4. Tap See Completed Downloads to see a list of tracks that have already been downloaded.

Latest Additions Playlist

When you view completed downloads, you're actually looking at an automatic playlist called Latest Additions. This playlist is also available on the Playlists screen.

Track currently downloading to device.

Canceling Downloads

You can cancel pending downloads. Any tracks that have already downloaded remain on your device.

1. While viewing active downloads, tap and hold the item that's currently downloading.

2. Tap Cancel Download.

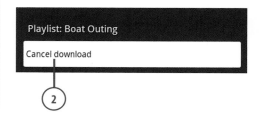

Searching for Music

I own a lot of music, and there are times when I need to search my music to find a particular song. You can just scroll through your song list on the Kindle Fire, but if you have thousands of songs, it's often easier to search for what you want to hear.

Your Kindle Fire can search music that's on your device as well as your music that's in the cloud.

Searching Your Music Collection

You can search for music on your device or your music that's in your Cloud Drive. (Before you can search for music on your device, you'll obviously need to download or sideload music to your device.)

You can search for playlists, artists, albums, or songs based on what you are currently viewing. For example, if you are looking at artists that are on your device and you start a search, your Kindle Fire will search for artists that match what you enter as your search.

1. Tap Device to search your Device or Cloud to search your Cloud Drive.

2. Tap Playlists, Artists, Albums, or Songs depending on what you want to search for.

3. Tap the Search icon.

4. Enter your search term in the Search box. Results appear as you type.

Shortcut to Searching the Music Store

If no matches are found for your search, you'll see a search icon where search results would normally appear. If you tap this search icon, your Kindle Fire will search the Music Store for the text you entered.

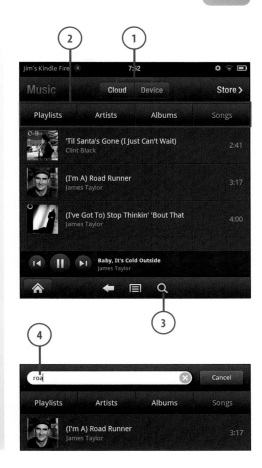

Playing Music

Your Kindle Fire can play music you've downloaded to the device, but it can also stream music from your Cloud Drive without requiring that you download the music to the device.

When you stream music, it requires a Wi-Fi connection because the music plays directly off of your Cloud Drive.

Music Controls in Quick Settings

If you tap Quick Settings (the icon next to the battery indicator) while music is playing, you see playback controls and the title and artist of the song that's currently playing. This is an easy way to control playback from any screen on the Kindle Fire.

Listening to Music

You can play music either through the stereo speakers built into the Kindle Fire or through headphones or an external speaker system. After you begin playing music, you can do other tasks on your Kindle Fire, such as reading books or magazines, and the music continues playing.

Streaming Music

The speed of your Wi-Fi network can vary. In order to avoid any delays in playback while streaming music, your Kindle Fire automatically buffers (loads) several tracks ahead for better performance.

1. Locate the song or songs that you want to hear.

2. Tap on a song to play the song and display the Now Playing screen.

3. Tap or drag the location slider to move to a particular point in the song. As you drag it, an indicator displays your position in the song.

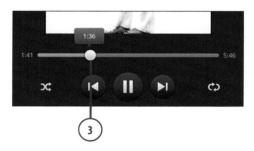

4. Tap Previous to move to the previous song.

5. Tap Next to move to the next song.

6. Tap or drag the Volume slider to adjust the volume of playback.

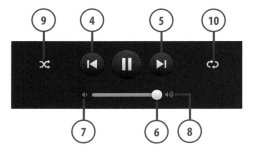

7. Tap the left side of the Volume slider to instantly mute the audio.

8. Tap the right side of the Volume slider to instantly change to full volume.

9. Tap Shuffle to play the songs in the Now Playing queue randomly. Tap it again to turn off shuffle playback. (I cover the Now Playing queue in the next section.)

10. Tap Repeat to repeat all of the songs in the Now Playing queue. Tap Repeat again to repeat only the currently playing song. A numeral 1 displays on the Repeat icon. (Tap it again to turn off repeat playback.)

Tap and Hold for More Options

While viewing the Now Playing screen, tap and hold the album art for a menu of other ways you can interact with your music, including the option to download tracks so that you can listen when you're not connected to Wi-Fi.

Playback Settings

From the Settings screen you can use your Kindle Fire's built-in equalizer to adjust how your music sounds. You can also choose to display music playback controls immediately after you unlock your Kindle File.

1. From any screen within your Music library, tap the Menu icon.

2. Tap Settings.

3. Tap Lock-screen Controls to enable the display of playback controls immediately upon unlocking your Kindle Fire.

Lock-screen Controls

The wording on the Kindle Fire implies that Lock-screen Controls enable the display of playback controls on the lock screen. In fact, the playback controls only display after you unlock your Kindle Fire.

4. Tap Enable Equalizer Modes to enable the Equalizer Mode drop-down.

5. Tap Equalizer Mode to change equalizer settings.

6. Tap an equalizer setting to change the equalizer mode.

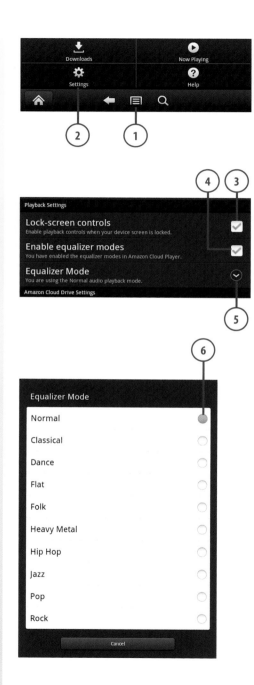

Using the Now Playing Queue

The Now Playing queue is kind of like a temporary playlist that you can use to queue up a series of tracks. There are a few ways that you can view the Now Playing queue. All assume that there are songs in the Now Playing queue.

Viewing from Quick Settings

You can view the Now Playing queue from Quick Settings while viewing almost any screen on the Kindle Fire.

1. Tap Quick Settings.

2. Tap the track and artist name.

Viewing from Library or Store

You can quickly access the Now Playing queue while you're viewing your Music library or the Amazon music store.

1. From the Home screen, tap Music.

2. Tap the track and artist name for the song that's currently playing.

Viewing from Music Menu

The menu in the Music library offers
a choice to view the Now Playing
queue.

1. From a screen in the Music library,
   tap the Menu icon.

2. Tap Now Playing.

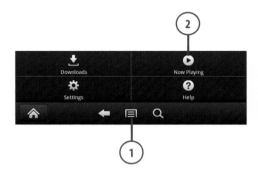

Viewing All Tracks in Now Playing

The default view of Now Playing displays the song that's currently playing along with album art and playback controls. You can view all of the
tracks in the Now Playing queue
from this view.

1. Tap the track list icon to display
   all tracks.

2. Tap the album art icon to return
   to the previous view.

Adding Songs to Now Playing

You can add one or more songs to the Now Playing queue. Songs are added to the end of the queue, so songs that you added first play first. Of course, if you are playing in shuffle mode, songs play in a random order.

1. Tap and hold a song in your music library and tap Add Song to Now Playing.

2. Tap and hold an album and tap Add Album to Now Playing.

3. Tap and hold an artist and tap Add Artist to Now Playing.

Adding Tracks Multiple Times

You can add tracks to the Now Playing queue multiple times. However, you are limited to adding 2,000 tracks to the Now Playing queue.

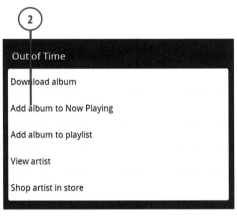

Removing Songs from the Now Playing Queue

You can remove one or more individual songs from the Now Playing queue.

1. From the Now Playing screen, tap the track list icon.

2. Tap and hold the song you want to remove.

3. Tap Remove from Now Playing to remove the song.

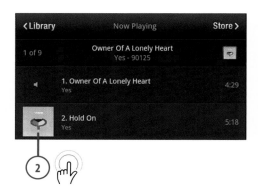

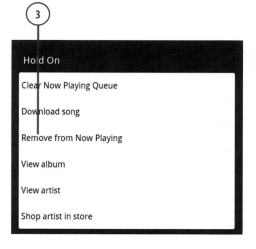

Clearing the Now Playing Queue

You can clear all tracks from the Now Playing queue.

1. From the Now Playing screen, tap the Menu icon.

2. Tap Clear Queue.

Another Way to Clear the Queue

You can also clear the Now Playing queue by tapping and holding on a song in the track list and tapping Clear Now Playing Queue.

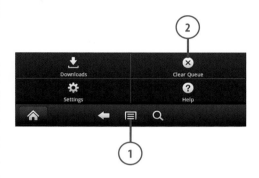

Managing Playlists

Playlists enable you to create a list of tracks that you want to play. You can create playlists on your device or in the cloud. If you create a playlist in the cloud, that playlist can be accessed from your computer or another device that can access your Cloud Drive.

Creating a Playlist

You create playlists on your device by first tapping the Device tab. If you tap the Cloud tab first, your playlist will be created on your Cloud Drive. Playlists that you create on your device can only contain songs that are on your device. Playlists that you create on your Cloud Drive can contain any of your music that is on your Cloud Drive.

1. From your Music library, tap Playlists.

2. Tap Cloud to create a playlist from tracks in your Cloud Drive or Device to create a playlist from tracks on your device.

3. Tap Create New Playlist.

4. Enter a name for your playlist.

5. Tap Save.

6. Add songs to your playlist by tapping the + sign next to the song.

7. Enter a song, album, or artist name to search for tracks.

8. Tap Done when finished adding songs.

Cannot Move Device Playlist to the Cloud

When you create a playlist on your device, that playlist can only contain songs that are on your device. You cannot move a playlist created on your device to the cloud.

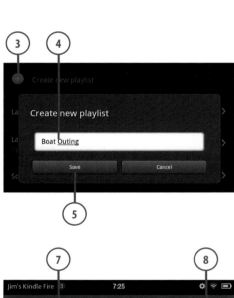

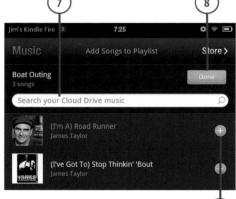

Editing a Playlist

After you've created a playlist and added your initial songs, you can add or remove songs by editing the playlist.

1. From the Playlists screen, tap your playlist.

2. Tap Edit.

3. Tap the minus sign to remove a song from the playlist.

4. Tap and hold the dots at the left edge of a song and drag it to a new position in the playlist to reorder songs.

5. Tap Add to add new songs using the same interface you used when creating the playlist.

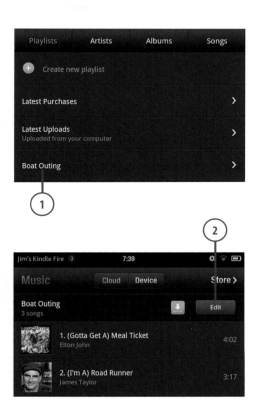

Adding Artists or Albums to a Playlist

Instead of adding songs one track at a time, you can add all songs by a particular artist or all songs in a particular album in one step.

1. Browse to the artist or album that you want to add to a playlist.

2. Tap and hold the artist or album.

3. Tap Add Album/Artist to Playlist.

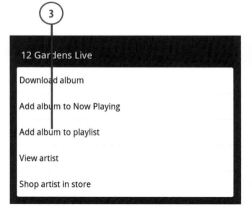

Adding Songs to Recent Playlist

If you've recently created a playlist, you see a menu item that enables you to add the album or artist to that specific playlist.

4. Tap the playlist to which you want to add the album or artist or tap Create New Playlist to create a new playlist.

5. If creating a new playlist, enter a name for the playlist.

6. Tap Save to save the new playlist.

Playing a Playlist

Playlists that are on your Kindle Fire can be played only on your Kindle Fire. When you create playlists in the cloud you can play them on your Kindle Fire or other devices that can access your Cloud Drive.

1. From your Music library, tap Playlists.

2. Tap Cloud to see playlists on your Cloud Drive or Device to see playlists on your Kindle Fire.

3. Tap the playlist you want to play.

4. Tap a song in the playlist to start playing from that song.

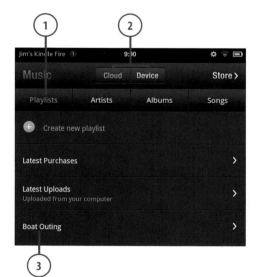

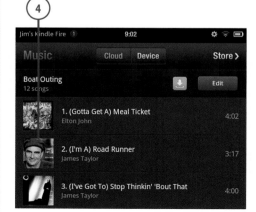

Downloading a Playlist

You can't play playlists that you create in your Cloud Drive unless you have an active Internet connection. If you want to play the playlist when you aren't connected, you need to download the playlist to your device.

1. From the Playlists screen, tap Cloud.

2. Tap the playlist that you want to download.

3. Tap the download icon to download the playlist to your device.

4. Tap Yes in the Download Playlist confirmation.

Downloaded Playlist

Downloaded playlists appear on the Device tab in the Playlists screen. Both the playlist and all songs in the playlist are downloaded.

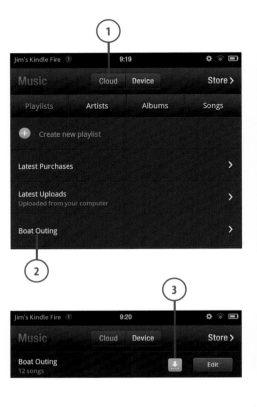

Renaming a Playlist

If you decide to change the name of a playlist, you can rename it from the Playlists screen.

1. From the Playlists screen, tap and hold the playlist that you want to rename.

2. Tap Rename Playlist.

3. Enter a new name for your playlist.

4. Tap Save.

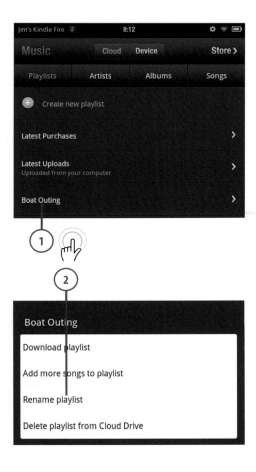

Deleting a Cloud Playlist

When you no longer want to keep a playlist, you can delete it. Deleting a playlist doesn't affect the tracks that you added to the playlist. It only removes the playlist.

When you delete a cloud playlist, it deletes that playlist from all devices that access your Cloud Drive.

1. From the Playlists screen, tap Cloud.

2. Tap and hold the playlist you want to delete.

3. Tap Delete Playlist from Cloud Drive.

4. Tap Yes to confirm the deletion.

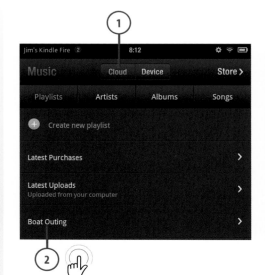

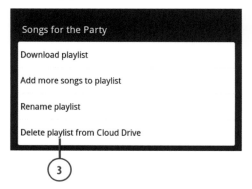

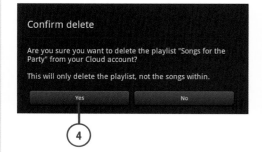

Removing a Device Playlist

You can also remove device playlists. If you originally downloaded the playlist from the cloud, removing it from your device does not affect the copy that's in the cloud.

1. From the Playlists screen, tap Device.

2. Tap and hold the playlist you want to remove from your device.

3. Tap Remove Playlist from Device.

4. Tap Yes to confirm the removal.

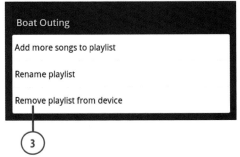

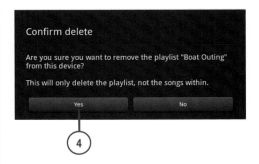

Buying New Music

You can purchase new music from Amazon's Music Store on your Kindle Fire. You can choose whether music that you purchase is only added automatically to your Cloud Drive or added to your Cloud Drive and then downloaded to your device.

Navigating the Music Store

The Music store is accessible from your Music library.

1. From any screen in your Music library, tap Store to go to the Music store.

2. Scroll through featured songs and albums.

3. Tap a category to see more music.

4. Tap Albums to see recommended albums.

5. Tap Songs to see recommended songs.

6. Scroll to view more recommendations.

7. Tap Search Music Store to search for music.

8. Tap any item to see details, sample tracks, and purchase music.

Sampling and Buying Songs

As you're browsing through the Music store, you can sample 30 seconds of songs or purchase songs.

1. Tap Songs to see a list of songs.

2. Tap a song or tap Play Sample to play a 30-second sample.

3. Tap the song price to purchase the song.

4. Tap and hold a song to access further shopping options.

5. Tap Shop Album to display the album that contains the song.

6. Tap Shop Artist to see all songs by that artist.

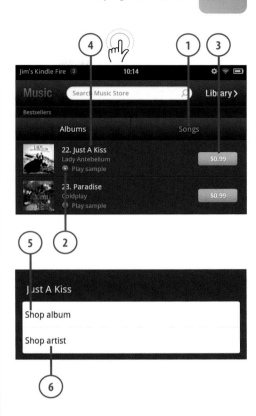

Sampling and Buying Albums

If you're the kind of music lover who prefers to buy albums, you can do that on your Kindle Fire as well.

1. Tap Albums to see a list of albums.

2. Tap an album to see details about the album.

3. Tap a song or tap the play button to play a 30-second sample.

Sampling Multiple Songs

When a 30-second sample finishes for one song, your Kindle Fire automatically starts playing a 30-second sample of the next song.

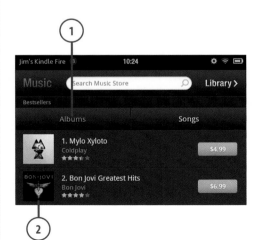

4. Tap the price of a song to purchase a single song.

5. Tap the album price to purchase the entire album.

6. Tap and hold a song to access more shopping options.

7. Tap Shop Artist to see all albums by the artist.

Website Only

Some albums and songs will say "Website Only" instead of allowing you to purchase them. Amazon does this when an album contains extra content that isn't compatible with your Kindle Fire. For example, if an album comes with a digital booklet of information about the album, the digital booklet displays "Website Only" instead of a price. Because the digital booklet is part of the album, you also won't be able to purchase the entire album from your Kindle Fire.

To purchase an album that says "Website Only" visit the Amazon MP3 store using a web browser. You can use Silk on your Kindle Fire if you'd prefer not to get up from the couch.

Returning to the Storefront

While browsing the store, you can tap Music in the upper-left corner of the screen to return to the storefront.

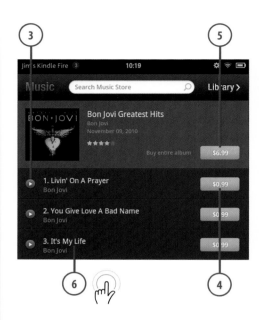

Changing Music Delivery Preference

When you purchase music, it is auto-matically added to your Cloud Drive. You can choose to have your music downloaded to your device instead, or you can choose both options.

1. While in the music store, tap the Menu icon.

2. Tap Settings.

3. Tap Delivery Preference.

4. Choose your preferred delivery method for music.

5. If you chose to have music added to your Cloud Drive, tap Automatic Downloads to have music that is added to your Cloud Drive automatically downloaded to your device.

Sideloading Music

You can sideload music files from your computer to your Kindle Fire. Music files must be in non-DRM AAC, MP3, MIDI, OGG, or WAV format before you sideload them.

Sideloading to Your Kindle Fire

You should copy music that you side-load to the Music folder.

1. Plug your Kindle Fire into your computer with a micro-USB cable and open the drive assigned to your Kindle Fire.

2. Copy your music files from your computer into the Music folder on your Kindle.

3. Disconnect your Kindle Fire from your computer.

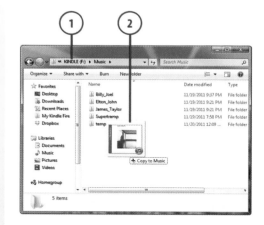

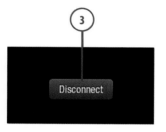

Create Folders in Music

It's best to keep your music files in the Music folder organized using subfolders. You can create any folder structure you like in the Music folder.

Watch Amazon Prime
videos for free

Watch your favorite
TV shows

Over 100,000
movies are available

In this chapter, you learn how to take advantage of the video capabilities of your Kindle Fire and how you can use your device to watch your own videos.

→ Navigating the Video Store
→ Working with Your Video Library
→ Sideloading Videos

Watching Video

Your Kindle Fire is an excellent device for watching videos. Amazon offers more than 100,000 movies and TV shows that you can watch immediately on your Kindle Fire, and if you're a Prime member, you can find thousands that you can watch instantly at no charge.

Navigating the Video Store

You can rent or purchase movies and TV shows from the Video Store. Amazon synchronizes your playback location automatically, so you can start watching on one device and finish on another.

If you're an Amazon Prime member (you get a free 30-day trial with your Kindle Fire), you can instantly watch many movies or TV shows without having to pay any additional money. (Not all videos are available for free Prime streaming.) These videos can only be streamed. You can't download them to your Kindle Fire, so you can't watch them if you're offline. On the other hand, videos that you rent or purchase can be streamed or downloaded to your device for offline watching.

Keep in mind that even if a video is offered for free streaming as an Amazon Prime member, you can still pay a rental fee (or purchase the video) and download it to your device if you choose.

Video Store or Library

When you are connected to Wi-Fi, tapping Video on the Home screen launches the Video Store. However, if you aren't connected to Wi-Fi, tapping Video takes you to your video library.

Browsing the Video Store

The Video Store is a single tap away from your Home screen.

1. Tap Video to access the Video Store.

2. Tap in the Search box to search for videos.

3. Scroll to view recommended titles.

4. Tap View All to view all Prime videos, Movies, or TV shows.

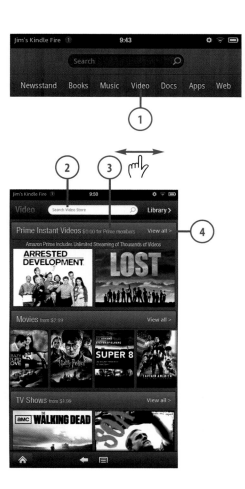

5. When viewing all, tap Movies to view movies or TV to view TV shows.

6. Tap Prime to view videos eligible for free streaming with a Prime membership or tap All to view all videos.

7. Scroll to see categories.

8. Tap a category to refine your view.

9. Tap Video to return to the Video Storefront.

Viewing Movie Details

The movie details screen provides an overview of a movie along with ways to explore additional titles that might interest you.

1. Tap a movie title in the Video Store.

2. Tap Watch Trailer to see the movie trailer.

3. Tap the name of an actor or director to see other movies featuring that person.

4. Scroll through recommended titles based on what other customers purchased.

5. Tap Rental & Purchase Details to view information about rental and purchase agreements from Amazon.

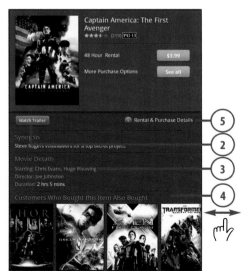

It's Not All Good

Rented Videos Might Expire Sooner Than You Think

When you rent a video, it typically expires 24 or 48 hours after you start watching it. However, if you initiate a download to your Kindle Fire, that will also start the clock on the expiration of the video. Therefore, if you download a video to your Kindle Fire, you'll need to pay careful attention to the expiration of the rental.

When you initiate a download, Amazon displays a notification informing you that you are about to start the rental period and will tell you how many hours you have to watch the movie.

Cannot See Review Details

You can view the review rating and the number of reviews from the movie details screen, but you can't read reviews on the movie. If you want to read reviews, you have to use a web browser.

Viewing TV Show Details

The only way to watch television is without the commercials. (My apologies to those of you in the advertising business.) I usually record the shows I want to watch, but even then, I have to fast forward through the ads, and doing so breaks up the continuity of the show I'm watching. A much better way to consume television content is to stream it from a content provider such as Amazon. Not only can you watch your favorite show in HD (and often with 5.1 surround sound), but you can do it without having to ever encounter a pause for advertising.

Amazon offers the ability to purchase single episodes of TV shows, but you can save a little money by purchasing an entire season. You can purchase a previous season and have access to all episodes immediately. You can also purchase the current season of your favorite show using what Amazon calls a "TV Pass." When you purchase a TV Pass, you get the season's episodes that have already aired immediately and new episodes of the season are made available to you usually the day after they air. You can cancel a TV Pass at any time and you aren't billed for future episodes.

1. Tap a TV show in the Video Store.

2. Tap More to read more details about the show.

3. Scroll to see available seasons.

4. Tap an episode to see details on that episode.

5. Tap a name to see more titles featuring that person.

6. Tap Rental & Purchase Details to see details on Amazon's purchase agreements.

7. Scroll to view recommended shows based on what other customers bought.

8. Tap More Episodes to return to the episode listing.

Networks Are People

You might notice that the network listed for House is David Shore. Shore is actually the producer of *House*, but because of the way Amazon's database is arranged, you will sometimes see strange entries like this.

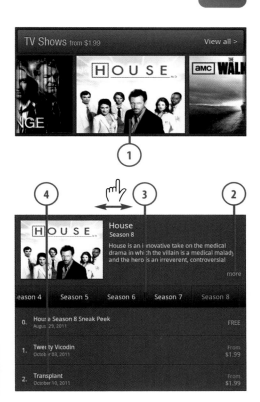

Renting or Purchasing a Movie

You can rent or purchase a movie on your Kindle Fire. You can then watch it on your Kindle Fire, on your TV, or another device.

It's Not All Good

Watching on a TV

You can't watch Amazon video that's on your Kindle Fire on a TV set. In order to watch Amazon TV that you rent or purchase on a TV set, you'll need to either have an Amazon app built into your TV set or you'll need to use a set-top box such as a Roku box.

Roku is widely considered to be the best set-top box for watching Amazon video (and other streaming video as well.) You can find out more about Roku boxes at www.roku.com.

Movies that you rent or purchase are available in your video library. I cover watching movies in "Working with Your Video Library" section.

1. Tap a movie to see movie details.

2. Tap the price to rent a standard definition (SD) version of the movie.

3. Tap See All to see all purchase options. This is where you'll have an option to purchase an HD version if one is available.

4. Tap a purchase option to complete your purchase or rental.

Changing Your Mind

If you decide you don't want to purchase the movie, you can tap Close.

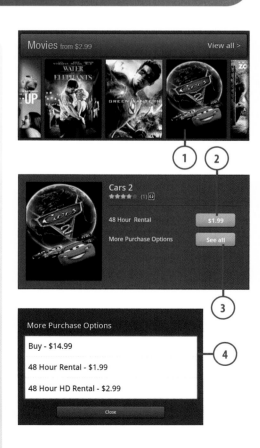

5. If you selected to purchase or rent an HD video, you might see a notification on buying HD videos. Click OK if you want to proceed with the HD purchase or rental.

6. Tap Confirm to confirm your movie rental or purchase.

Renting HD Videos

I frequently start watching a video on my TV in HD and then finish watching it on my Kindle Fire. Therefore, I prefer to always rent or purchase videos in HD. Even though your Kindle Fire isn't HD, it can play HD videos; they're just in SD.

In case you were wondering, there isn't a way to watch videos on your TV that are stored on your Kindle Fire.

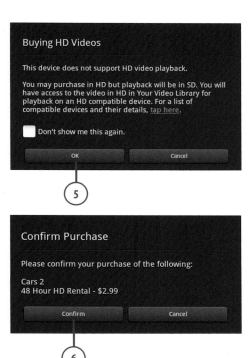

Buying TV Shows

Television shows are only available for purchase. You cannot rent a TV episode. TV shows that you purchase are available in your video library. I cover watching TV shows in the "Working with Your Video Library" section.

1. Tap a TV show from the Video Store.

2. Select a season.

3. Tap the episode you want to purchase.

4. Tap the price to purchase the episode in SD.

5. Tap See All to see additional purchase options.

6. Tap a purchase option.

7. If you selected an HD version and you see the Buying HD Videos dialog, tap OK.

8. Tap Confirm to confirm your purchase.

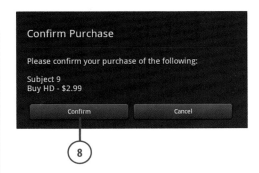

Buying Seasons

Amazon also offers an option to purchase an entire season of a TV show at a discounted price. However, this option isn't available in the Video Store on your Kindle Fire. To purchase all episodes in a particular season, visit www.amazon.com/instantvideo on your computer. You can then watch those videos on your Kindle Fire if you want.

Disabling the HD Purchase Warning

You can disable the warning dialog that appears when you purchase or rent HD videos on your Kindle Fire.

1. From the video library, tap the Menu icon.

2. Tap Settings.

3. Tap Disable HD Purchase Warning to place a check in the box.

Working with Your Video Library

Your video library contains video items that you own as well as video rentals from the Video Store. Items that you own will always be available in your video library unless you permanently delete them. Items that you rent appear in your video library only during the rental period, after which time they disappear.

Your Video Library

You can delete videos from your video library by visiting the Your Video Library page at www.amazon.com/gp/video/library. Simply click on a video and then click the Delete link.

Watching a Movie or TV Show

You can stream movies and TV episodes from the cloud to your Kindle Fire as long as you have an active Wi-Fi connection. You can also watch videos that you've downloaded to your device.

1. From the Video store, tap Library.

2. Tap Movies or TV to locate the video you want to watch.

3. Tap Cloud to see movies in the cloud or tap Device to see videos you've downloaded.

4. Tap By Recent to sort your videos by when they were added to your library.

5. Tap By Name to sort your videos by name.

6. Tap a video you'd like to watch.

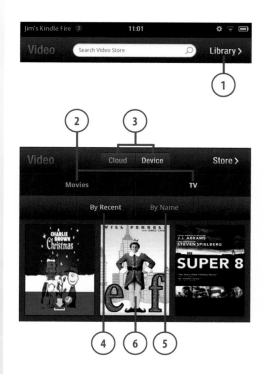

7. Tap Watch Now to watch the video. You must remain connected to Wi-Fi while watching.

8. Tap Download to download the video for watching while you are not connected to Wi-Fi.

9. While a video is playing, tap the center of the screen to display controls.

10. Tap Play/Pause to pause playback and resume playback.

11. Drag the slider to move to a specific point in time.

12. Tap the skip back button to move backward 10 seconds.

13. Drag the volume slider to adjust the volume.

14. Tap the left side of the volume slider to mute audio.

15. Tap the right side of the volume slider to change to full volume.

16. Tap Back to return to the details screen for the video.

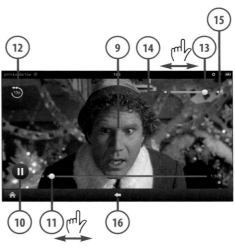

Downloading Videos

Videos that are in the cloud must be downloaded to your device if you want to play them when you are not connected to Wi-Fi.

1. From your video library, tap Cloud.

2. Tap and hold the video that you want to download.

3. Tap Download to download the video to your device.

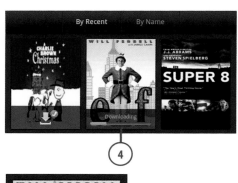

4. A progress bar is displayed while the video downloads.

5. When the movie has finished downloading, an icon appears on the video's thumbnail.

Removing a Downloaded Video

After you've watched a video, you might want to remove it from your device so that it doesn't take up space. If you own the video, you can download it again at any time.

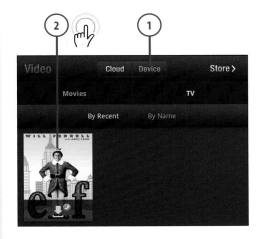

1. From your video library, tap Device to see videos on your device.

2. Tap and hold the video you want to delete from your device.

3. Tap Delete Download to delete the movie.

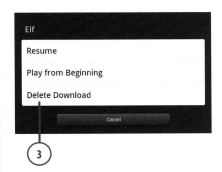

Deleted Video Still Appears

Videos that you delete might still appear on your device until you take some action (such as switching to another view) that causes the video library to refresh.

Sideloading Videos

Digital video comes in a huge assortment of formats, enough to make your head spin. The good news for you is that your Kindle Fire only supports two different formats; MP4 (or MPEG 4) and VP8. (You can pretty much ignore VP8 for now because almost no one uses it.) You might also hear MP4 video referred to as *H.264* (pronounced "h dot two sixty-four"). H.264 is most often used to compress and decompress digital audio and video in MP4 format. Compression is necessary, because video files can take up a *huge* amount of space, and compression formats like MP4 help keep it all manageable.

If you have video that you'd like to play on your Kindle Fire, you can easily convert it to an MP4 video using free software.

Converting Videos for Kindle Fire

As I said, before you can play a video on your Kindle Fire, you need to convert it to a suitable format. The easiest way to do this is to use Handbrake, a free application you can download from www.handbrake.fr.

1. Start Handbrake.

2. Open the Source menu and click Video File. Click OK on the warning dialog that appears.

3. Select a video file you want to convert and click Open.

4. Select a folder and enter a filename for the converted video.

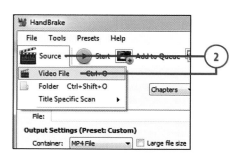

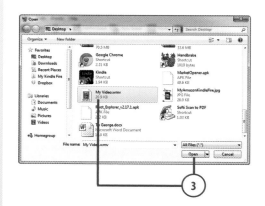

5. Select High Profile in the preset list.

6. Select None in the Anamorphic drop-down.

7. Change the Height to 600. (Handbrake automatically changes this number after you enter it based on your source video size.)

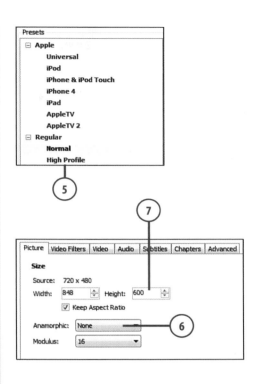

Widescreen Video

By setting the height to 600, you ensure that widescreen video fills the entire screen on your Kindle Fire. If your source video isn't widescreen, you don't need to set the height.

---

8. Click Start to start the conversion process.

Conversion Time

After the conversion percentage reaches 100%, Handbrake seems to stall for a while. This is normal. After Handbrake reports that the conversion is finished in the status bar, you can sideload the converted video to your Kindle.

Copying Video to Your Kindle Fire

To sideload videos from your computer to your Kindle Fire, copy or paste them into the Kindle Fire's Video folder.

1. Connect your Kindle Fire to your computer using a micro-USB cable.

2. Open the drive for your Kindle Fire.

3. Copy your video into the Video folder.

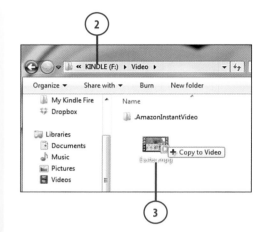

Watching Sideloaded Videos

Sideloaded videos don't actually show up in your Video library. Instead, you need to use the Gallery to watch them.

1. From your Home screen, tap Apps.

2. Tap Gallery to start the Gallery app.

3. Tap your video to select it.

4. Tap your video again to play it.

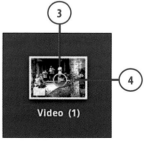

Deleting Sideloaded Video

To delete sideloaded videos, you can simply delete the files from your Kindle Fire's Video folder. You can also delete them within the Gallery app.

1. In Gallery, tap to select the video you want to delete.

2. Tap the Menu icon.

3. Tap Delete.

4. Tap Confirm Delete.

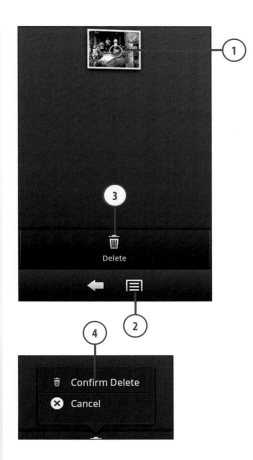

Get plenty of cool apps to enhance the capabilities of your Kindle Fire

In this chapter, you'll learn how to find and install apps from Amazon's Appstore for Android and you'll learn how to manage and use those apps.

Installing and Using Apps

Your Kindle Fire comes with 10 apps already installed and provides access to Amazon's Appstore for Android so that you can get other apps. Apps that are available from the Appstore for Android on your Kindle Fire have been tested for compatibility with the Kindle Fire.

The Appstore for Android contains a wide assortment of apps. You can find apps for cooking, education, health & fitness, reference apps, shopping apps, sports apps, and much more. Some of these apps are free, and some are not. Some of these apps are good apps, and some are not. Unfortunately, you can't try an app before you buy it, so it's a good idea to read the reviews on an app to decide if it's worth the price.

Your App Library

Your app library contains applications that you have downloaded to your device as well as applications that you have purchased but not downloaded. When you purchase an app from the Appstore for Android, the app is added to your app library, but before you can use the app, you'll need to download and install it.

Included Free Apps

Amazon includes some free apps in your app library. These apps don't come preinstalled on your Kindle Fire. You'll see them when you tap the Cloud tab in your app library.

Browsing Your App Library

All of your apps are available by browsing your app library.

1. From the Home screen, tap Apps.

2. Tap Cloud to see all of the apps you've purchased, both on your device and in the cloud.

3. Tap Device to see only those apps that are installed on your device.

4. Tap By Recent to sort your apps by when they were added to your library.

5. Tap By Title to sort your apps by title.

6. Scroll to see more apps.

7. Tap the Search icon to search your app library.

Installing a Purchased App

Apps that you've purchased but not yet installed display a download arrow icon in your app library.

1. Tap the app that you would like to install.

2. Tap Install to install the app.

3. Wait for your app to download and install.

4. Tap Open to open the app or tap it from your app library.

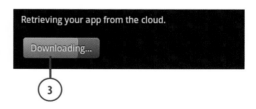

It's Not All Good

Installing Apps from Unknown Sources

Your Kindle Fire provides the ability to install third-party apps from sources other than the Appstore for Android. However, I advise against doing so for a couple of reasons. First of all, many of the apps I tested crashed my Kindle Fire or caused unpredictable behavior. Secondly, Android apps are a common source of Android viruses, and because the Kindle Fire is directly tied to your Amazon account, the risk of installing apps from unknown sources is simply too great to ignore.

Installing Multiple Apps at Once

If you have many apps to install, you can easily install several at the same time.

1. From your app library, tap Store.

2. Tap the Menu icon.

3. Tap My Apps.

4. Tap Install next to one or more apps to queue them for download and install. You can queue up to five installs.

Cannot Cancel Queued Downloads

You cannot cancel the installation of an app that has been queued for download and install. If you queue an application by mistake, you can uninstall it as described later in this chapter in the section "Uninstalling an App."

Adding an App to Favorites

You can add an app to your Favorites shelf for easier access. You'll find more information on using and organizing your Favorites in "The Home Screen" section of Chapter 1, "Getting Started with the Kindle Fire."

1. Tap Device to see only those apps that you've installed.

2. Tap and hold the app that you want to add to Favorites.

3. Tap Add to Favorites.

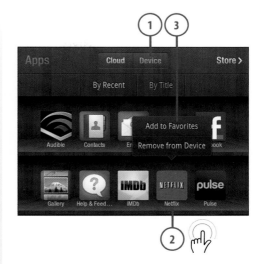

Uninstalling an App

Uninstalling an app removes it from your device. You can reinstall the app at a later time if you want without having to pay for it again.

1. Tap Device to see only those apps that you've installed.

2. Tap and hold the app that you want to uninstall.

3. Tap Remove from Device to uninstall the app.

4. Tap OK to confirm.

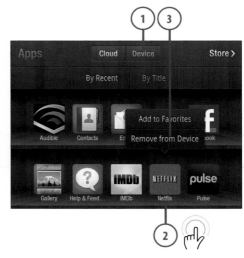

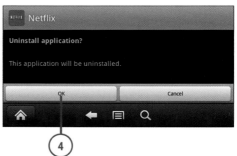

5. Tap OK when informed that the app has been uninstalled.

Cannot Uninstall Preinstalled Apps

Audible, Contacts, Email, Facebook, Gallery, Help & Feedback, IMDb, Pulse, Quickoffice, and Shop are all pre-installed apps, and you cannot uninstall them from your Kindle Fire.

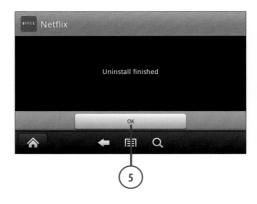

Updating an Application

When an update is available for an application, you can install the update from My Apps.

1. From your app library, tap Store.

2. Tap the Menu icon.

3. Tap My Apps.

4. Tap Update Available.

5. Tap Update to install the update.

The Appstore

You can purchase new apps for your Kindle Fire in the Appstore. When you browse the store from your Kindle Fire, all of the apps listed in the store are compatible with your device.

Appstore for Android from Web Browser

You can access the Appstore for Android on your computer using a web browser, but not all of the apps listed in the Web interface are compatible with your Kindle Fire. When you view an app via the Web interface, you'll see a checkmark for your Kindle Fire, as shown here, if the app is compatible.

An app compatible with the Kindle Fire.

Browsing Apps

The Appstore offers plenty of tools that make shopping for apps easier.

1. Amazon offers a paid app for free every day. Tap to install the app.

2. Scroll to select a category of app or to view recommended apps.

3. Scroll to view more apps.

Viewing and Purchasing Apps

You can view details of an app before deciding to purchase an app.

1. Tap an app that you are interested in.

2. Tap Product Info to view general information about the app.

3. Tap Photos to view screenshots of the app.

Zoom in on Screenshots

Tap a screenshot to zoom in. You can then swipe through the screenshots.

---

4. Tap Reviews to read reviews.

5. Tap Create Your Own Review to review the app.

6. Scroll to read additional reviews.

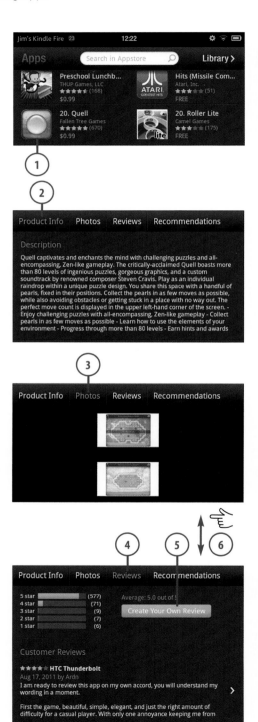

7. Tap Recommendations to see what others purchased after viewing the app.

8. Tap Save to add the app to your Saved for Later list.

9. Tap the price to purchase and install the app.

It's Not All Good

Crashing Apps

Apps are software, and like it or not, all software has bugs in it. (A software bug is a problem in the software's programming code that causes it to behave in an unexpected way.) Some bugs will cause the app to behave strangely or in an unpredictable way. Other bugs are more serious and can crash an app making it stop without notice.

If an app that you are using disappears and you are instantly returned to the Home screen, it means that the app crashed. Unlike on your laptop or desktop, you don't see a message when an app crashes on your Kindle Fire. Instead, the app just disappears. When this happens, restart the app and all should be fine. However, if you still encounter problems after restarting, try clearing the app's data. See "Clearing Application Data" later in this chapter to find out how to clear an app's data.

Viewing Saved or Recently Viewed Apps

You can view apps you've added to your Saved for Later list. You can also view apps that you've recently viewed.

1. From the app store, tap the Menu icon.

2. Tap More.

3. Tap Saved for Later to view apps you've saved.

4. Tap Recently Viewed to view a list of apps you've viewed recently.

Viewing Subscriptions

Some magazines are available for the Kindle Fire as apps instead of through the Newsstand. For example, the *WIRED* magazine and *The New Yorker* magazine both have apps for accessing their content. These magazines are typically offered as a free app, but in order to read the content, you must subscribe via the app. You can view the status and manage these subscriptions from the Appstore.

1. From the Appstore, tap the Menu icon.

2. Tap My Subscriptions.

3. Tap a subscription to view details or manage the subscription.

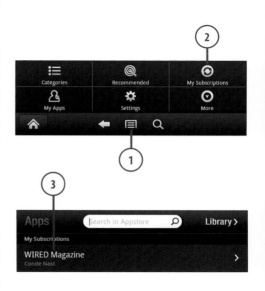

Changing a Subscription Period

Most subscriptions offer the option of subscribing on a monthly or an annual basis. You can decide which period you'd prefer.

1. While viewing subscription details, tap Change Subscription Period.

2. Tap a new subscription period.

3. Tap Save Changes.

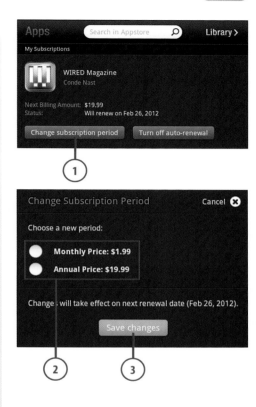

Turning Off Auto-Renewal

By default, subscriptions automatically renew when they expire. You can turn off auto-renewal.

1. While viewing subscription details, tap Turn off Auto-Renewal.

2. Tap Turn off Auto-Renewal.

Reactivating Auto-Renewal
After you've turned off auto-renewal, you can turn it back on by tapping Turn on Auto-Renewal in the subscription details.

Changing Subscription Privacy Preferences

By default, Amazon allows subscription publishers to use your name and billing address for marketing. You can choose what information you want Amazon to share with publishers.

1. While viewing subscription details, tap Change Privacy Preferences.

2. Uncheck items you don't want to share and check information you do want to share with publishers.

3. Tap to check Use These Settings for Future Newspaper & Magazine Purchases if you want to use your selections as the default from now on.

4. Tap Save Preferences.

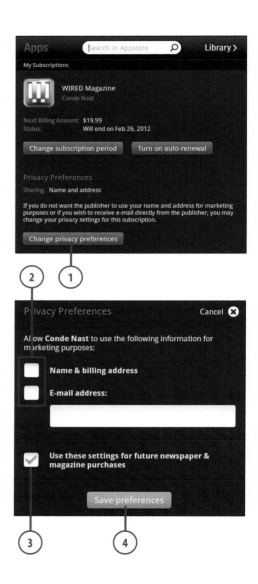

Application Settings

In some cases, you might need to force an application to close if it's misbehaving. You might also want to clear data that an application is caching or storing. For example, if an app is behaving unpredictably even after you force close it and relaunch it, the app might have some corrupted data in its cache or database.

You can force close apps and delete app data from the Application Settings screen.

Force Stopping an Application

If an app is causing problems on your Kindle Fire, or if an app hangs and becomes unresponsive, you can force the app to close. This is called *force stopping* an app.

1. Tap Quick Settings.

2. Tap More.

3. Tap Applications.

4. Tap Filter By.

5. Tap All Applications.

6. Scroll to locate the app you want to stop.

7. Tap the app that's frozen.

8. Tap Force Stop to stop the app.

9. Tap OK in the confirmation dialog to force stop the app.

Running Applications

When you select Running Applications in Application Settings, you'll only see Amazon apps. You won't see any third-party apps.

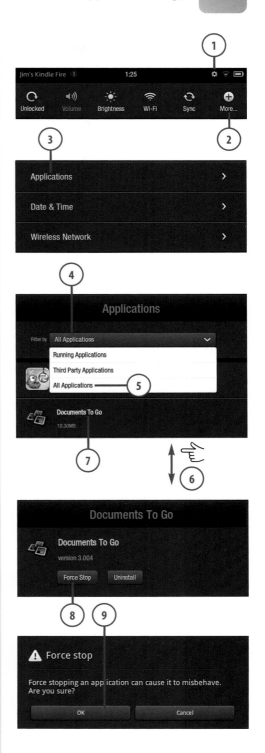

SHOULD YOU WORRY ABOUT CLOSING APPS?

When you finish with an app on your Kindle Fire, you tap the Home button to get back to the Home screen. When you do this, the app remains running in the background. After a while, you might have dozens of apps that are running in the background on your Kindle Fire.

On a laptop or desktop computer, you wouldn't want to have a large number of applications running when you're not using them, because those applications use resources on your computer and can slow it down and cause other problems. However, things are different on your Kindle Fire. The Kindle Fire's operating system is designed to account for many apps running that aren't currently in use. When you switch away from an app, it enters a state where it doesn't do anything at all. Some apps are designed to periodically "wake up" for a second or two to check for content or to perform some other task, but they go back to sleep once that task is complete.

The bottom line is that you don't have to worry about apps running in the background on your Kindle Fire. They won't use more battery power and they won't consume resources like an application would on your laptop or desktop computer.

Clearing Application Data

If an app is not working properly even after you force stop it, it's possible that the app's data are corrupt. You can clear an app's data in Application settings.

1. While viewing all apps in Application settings, tap the app whose data you'd like to clear.

2. Tap Clear Data.

3. Tap OK in the confirmation dialog.

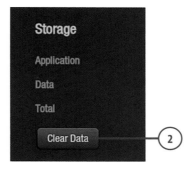

It's Not All Good

Clearing Data Clears Everything

When you clear data for an app, you clear all settings and any other data that the app has stored. The next time you launch the app, it starts with the default settings. Make sure that you don't clear data unless you're sure that you don't need any information that the app is storing.

If you continue to have problems with an app after you clear its data, it's possible that what you are experiencing is a bug in the app. You can look at the app's page in the Appstore for Android to see if there is a way to contact the developer and provide feedback. Many Android developers are thrilled to get that kind of feedback from users, and most are willing to fix problems if possible.

Indispensable Apps

Amazon includes 10 apps on your Kindle Fire when it ships. Some of these are great apps that you might find yourself using often, and there are other apps available in the Appstore that I consider to be indispensable. You need to download some of these apps from the Appstore, but all of them are free.

I have no doubt that I've left out apps that you might find indispensable, so please feel free to suggest additional apps to share with readers on this book's website at www.myamazonkindlefire.com and I'll be sure to spread the word.

Listening to Audible Books

Audible is Amazon's app for listening to audio books. There are more than 100,000 audio books and other programs available from Audible, and all are available from the Audible app on your Kindle Fire.

You can shop for audio books within the Audible app, but the interface is awkward. I prefer to shop for audio books from within a web browser on my computer.

Audible Plans
Audible plans do cost money. The cheapest plan is $14.95 per month, but you get one free audio book per month for that price. You can also save a little by paying for an entire year.

1. Launch the Audible app.

2. Tap Sign In to log in with an existing Audible account or tap I'm New to Audible to create an account.

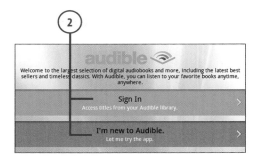

3. After signing in, tap a title in your library to download it to your Kindle Fire.

4. Although you can wait until it is fully downloaded, while a title is downloading, you can press play to begin playing it immediately.

5. Tap Pause to pause playback.

6. Tap the Bookmark icon to save a bookmark that you can return to easily.

7. Tap Details for details on the audio book.

8. Tap Chapters to see a list of chapters.

9. Tap Bookmarks to see a list of your bookmarks.

10. Tap the Menu icon for additional options.

11. Tap Share to post onto Facebook or send an email to someone about the book you're listening to.

12. Tap Sleep to set a sleep timer that will stop playback of the book after a certain time period.

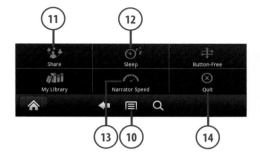

13. Tap Narrator Speed to change the speed at which the audio book is played.

14. Tap Quit to quit the Audible app.

Why Quit?

I said earlier that most apps don't offer an option to quit the app. The Audible app does, because any audio book that you are listening to will continue playing if you switch to another screen or another app. If you want to stop an Audible book from playing, you should either stop it from within the Audible app or quit the Audible app instead of just switching away from it.

Returning to an Audio Book

The Audible app saves your listening position so that you can return to the same point in your audio book.

Gallery

The Gallery is a convenient app for viewing videos and pictures. There are other apps available for viewing multimedia, but Gallery is an Android staple.

Copy any pictures you want to view to the Pictures folder on your Kindle Fire. If you want your pictures to show up in a named gallery in the Gallery app, copy the pictures into a folder by that name.

1. Launch the Gallery app.

2. Tap a picture, video, or folder.

3. Tap a picture to view the picture.

4. Tap and hold to select one or more pictures so that you can rotate or crop the picture.

5. Tap the view icon to toggle between viewing all pictures and viewing pictures grouped by date and time.

6. Tap Gallery to return to the gallery showing all pictures.

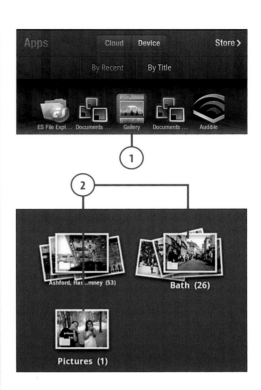

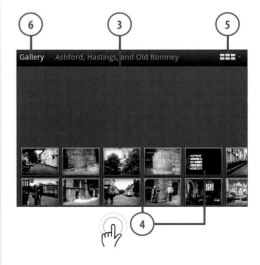

Pandora

Pandora Internet Radio is a service whereby you enter the name of a song or an artist and Pandora finds other songs that you'll almost certainly like. It's a great way to discover new music.

1. Launch Pandora.

2. Sign in or create a new Pandora account.

3. Select an existing radio station to start playing that station.

4. Tap the Menu icon and tap Create Station to create a new station.

5. While a station is playing, tap Pause to pause playback.

6. Tap Next to skip to a new song.

7. Tap thumbs up to tell Pandora you like the current song.

8. Tap thumbs down to tell Pandora you don't like the current song and skip to the next song.

9. Tap the station's icon to return to your list of stations.

Buy Stuff You Like

While listening to Pandora, you can tap the Menu icon and tap Buy to purchase the song or the album that you are currently listening to.

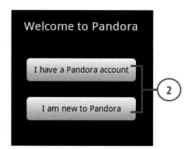

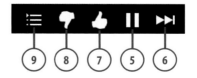

Warning About Data Usage

The Pandora app warns you about data usage when you first launch it. It does this because the developers knew that it was most likely to be used on Android phones that have cellular data plans. However, since your Kindle Fire uses Wi-Fi, you don't need to worry about data usage unless your Internet service provider charges you based upon how much bandwidth you use.

ES File Explorer

ES File Explorer is a convenient way to view files that are stored on your Kindle Fire. It's the easiest way I've found to locate files you downloaded from the Internet, attachments you've saved from emails, and other files stored on your Kindle Fire's internal memory. In fact, you can also use it to access files on other computers on your network.

Finding ES Fire Explorer

ES File Explorer isn't listed in your app library by default. You'll need to search the Appstore for it.

It's Not All Good

Be Careful When Deleting or Renaming Files

Because ES File Explorer enables you to see files that are part of your Kindle Fire's operating system, it's possible for you to corrupt your Kindle Fire if you delete or rename a system file. Be careful!

If you do accidentally corrupt your Kindle Fire's operating system, you can recover it by tapping Reset to Factory Defaults on the Device Settings screen. (See Device Information in Chapter 1 for details on the Device Settings screen.) However, resetting your device causes you to lose anything stored on the device that's not backed up somewhere else.

1. Launch ES File Explorer.

2. Tap a folder to see the contents of the folder.

3. Tap a file to open the file in an app capable of viewing the file.

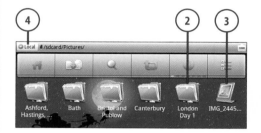

ES File Explorer and Viewing Files

ES File Explorer includes ES Image Browser and other mini-apps that can view certain file types. When you tap a file type that ES File Explorer can view natively, you might be asked to pick a program to use to open the file. The choice is yours as it really doesn't matter.

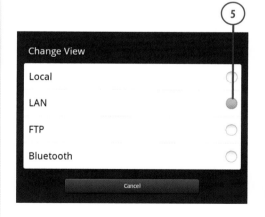

4. To view folders on another computer on your network, tap Local in the upper-left of the main screen.

5. Tap LAN.

6. Tap the up arrow to display the status bar.

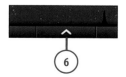

7. Tap the Menu icon and tap New.

8. Tap Server.

9. Enter the computer name you want to add.

10. Enter a username and password to log onto the computer.

11. Enter a display name if you want.

12. Tap OK to add the server.

Opening Unsupported Files in ES File Explorer

If you attempt to open a file type in ES File Explorer that isn't supported on your Kindle Fire, ES File Explorer typically displays a black screen instead of displaying the file. In these cases, just tap Back to return to the interface.

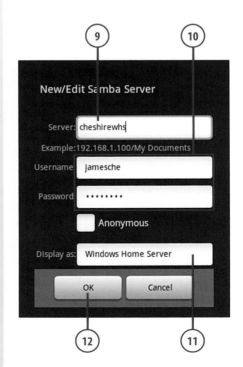

View and save
attachments

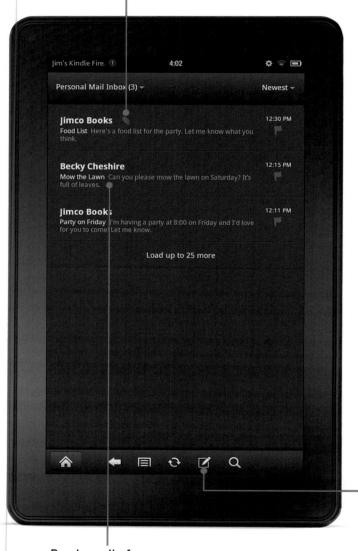

Jim's Kindle Fire ①   4:02   ⚙ 🛜 🔋

Personal Mail Inbox (3) ▾   Newest ▾

Jimco Books 📎   12:30 PM
Food List Here's a food list for the party. Let me know what you
think.   🚩

Becky Cheshire   12:15 PM
Mow the Lawn Can you please mow the lawn on Saturday? It's
full of leaves.   🚩

Jimco Books   12:11 PM
Party on Friday I'm having a party at 8:00 on Friday and I'd love
for you to come. Let me know.   🚩

Load up to 25 more

🏠   ⬅   ☰   ⟳   ✎   🔍

Create
new email
messages

Read emails from a
unified inbox for all of
your email accounts

In this chapter, you'll learn how to set up email accounts on your Kindle Fire, how to check your email, and how to send email. You'll also learn how to deal with email attachments.

9

→ Email Accounts
→ Managing Your Email Inbox
→ Reading Email
→ Sending Messages
→ Working with Email Contacts

Reading and Sending Email

Your Kindle Fire comes with an app for email and an app for managing your email contacts. You can read your email, send emails, and even view email attachments.

Your Kindle Fire supports various email services including Gmail, Hotmail, Yahoo!, and POP3 and IMAP servers. You can set up multiple email accounts on your Kindle Fire. You can then either access each inbox individually or you can use the unified inbox to see all of your messages from all accounts on one screen.

Email Accounts

The first step in using email on your Kindle Fire is setting up your email account. Kindle Fire supports basic accounts (Gmail, Yahoo!, Hotmail, and AOL) as well as IMAP and POP3 accounts that most Internet service providers offer their subscribers.

Check Help for Information

While on the account setup screen, tap the Menu icon and tap Help for settings you can use for many common email providers.

Adding a Basic Account

If you have a Gmail, Yahoo!, Hotmail (Windows Live), or AOL email account, you can easily configure it on your Kindle Fire.

1. Start the Email app from the Kindle Fire's Apps page.

2. Tap Start.

3. Tap your email provider from the list: Gmail, Yahoo, Hotmail, or AOL.

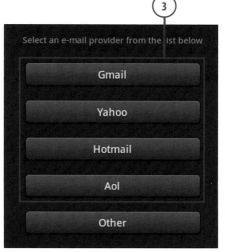

4. Enter your username. (This is typically your full email address.)

5. Enter your password.

6. Tap Next.

7. Enter your name.

8. Enter the display name for this
account on your Kindle Fire.

9. Check the box if you want new
email messages to use this
account by default.

Gmail Contacts
If you're setting up a Gmail
account, you'll have the option to
import your contacts if you want.

10. Tap View Your Inbox.

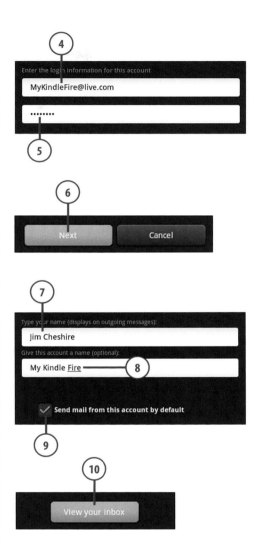

Adding an Additional Email Account

The start screen that shows you a collection of buttons for setting up a new email account only appears when you haven't set up any email accounts. The steps for setting up additional accounts are slightly different.

1. Launch the Email app.

2. Tap the Menu icon.

3. Tap Accounts.

4. Tap the Menu icon.

5. Tap Add Account and follow the steps as they are described in the previous section, "Adding a Basic Account," or in the following section, "Adding a POP3 or IMAP Account."

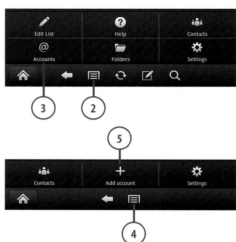

Adding a POP3 or IMAP Account

You can set up your Kindle Fire to read and send email from a POP3 or IMAP account.

1. From the email provider list, tap Other.

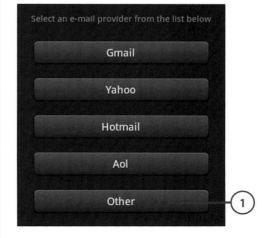

2. Enter your username.

3. Enter your password.

4. Tap Next.

5. Tap POP 3 to set up a POP3 account.

6. Tap IMAP to set up an IMAP account.

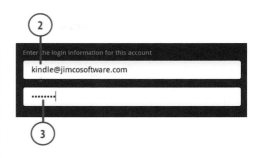

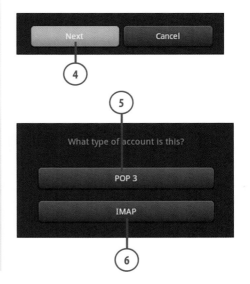

It's Not All Good

No Exchange Support

The built-in email app doesn't support Microsoft Exchange servers. You can get an app called Exchange By TouchDown that allows you to configure your Exchange email on your Kindle Fire, but the app carries a relatively steep price of $12.99. If you want to try it out to see if it fits your needs, you can download the free version and use it for 30-days.

Configuring a POP3 Account

After you select POP3 as your account type, you need to configure the account. Most of this information is already filled in based on information you've already entered, but you should check it to ensure that it's correct.

If you're unsure about a setting, check with your email provider.

1. Enter your username.

2. Enter your password.

3. Enter the address of your POP3 server.

4. Tap Security Type and select a security type if necessary.

5. Tap Authentication Type and select the authentication type.

6. Enter a new port number if required. Note that the existing port number is based on the security type, and it's likely correct already.

7. Tap Next.

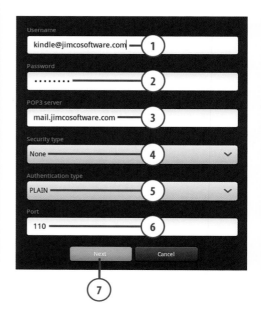

8. Enter your SMTP (outgoing server) address.

9. Tap Security Type and select a security type.

10. Enter a port number if required.

11. If your SMTP server requires you to log in (most do), check Require Sign-In.

12. Tap Authentication Type and select the authentication type. Leave it set to Automatic if you're unsure.

13. Enter your username.

14. Enter your password.

15. Tap Next.

16. Tap Folder Poll Frequency and select how often you want to check for new mail.

17. Tap Next.

18. Enter the name that you want to display on emails sent from this account.

19. Enter a display name for this account on your Kindle Fire.

20. Check the box if you want email to be sent from this account by default.

21. Tap View Your Inbox to go to your inbox.

POP3 Emails Remain on Server

Unlike many POP3 email clients, the Kindle Fire's email app does not remove emails from your server when you read them. Therefore, if you have your email account configured on another device or computer, you can still see your mail on that device after reading it on your Kindle Fire. Even if you delete an email message from your Kindle Fire, the email message remains on the server by default.

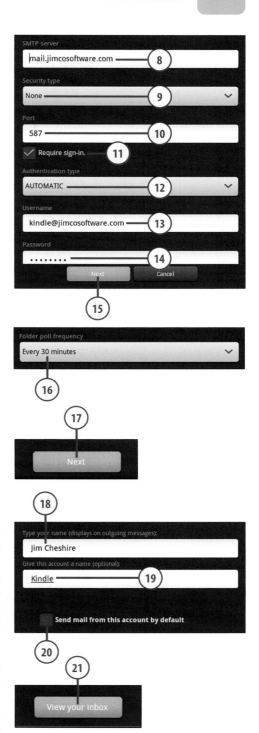

Configuring an IMAP Account

After you select IMAP as your account type, you need to configure the account. Most of this information is already filled in based on information you've already entered, but you should check it to ensure that it's correct.

If you're unsure about a setting, check with your email provider.

1. Enter your username.

2. Enter your password.

3. Enter your IMAP server's address.

4. Tap Security Type and select a security type.

5. Tap Authentication Type and select an authentication type.

6. Change the port if required.

7. Scroll down to reveal additional options.

8. Enter an IMAP Path Prefix if necessary. (This can be left as-is in most cases.)

9. Check Wi-Fi to enable compression if you want. If you have metered Internet, this can save some bandwidth. (Mobile and Other aren't applicable on the Kindle Fire.)

10. Tap Next.

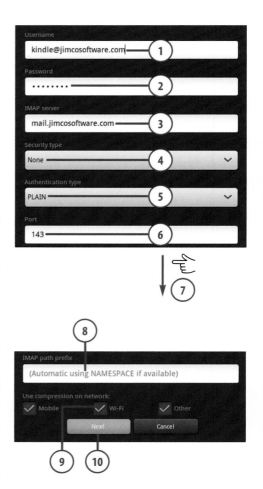

11. Enter your SMTP (outgoing server) address.

12. Tap Security Type and select a security type.

13. Change the port if necessary.

14. Tap Require Sign-In if your SMTP server requires you to sign in.

15. Tap Authentication Type and select an authentication type if necessary.

16. Enter your username.

17. Enter your password.

18. Tap Next.

19. Tap Folder Poll Frequency and select how often you would like to check for new email.

20. Tap Next.

21. Enter a name to display on emails sent from this account.

22. Enter a display name for this account on your Kindle Fire.

23. Check the box to have emails sent from this account by default.

24. Tap View Your Inbox to be taken to your inbox.

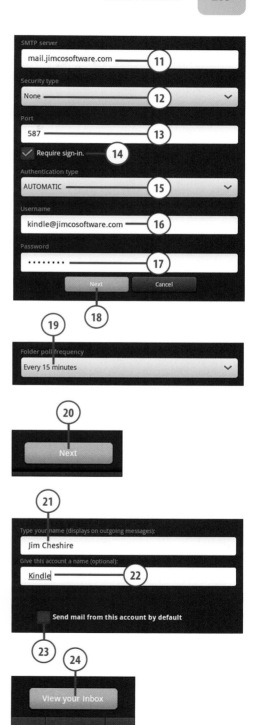

Removing an Account

You can remove an account from your Kindle Fire if you no longer want to read email from that account on your device.

1. While viewing your inbox, tap the Menu icon.

2. Tap Accounts to access the Accounts screen.

3. Tap and hold the account you want to remove.

4. Tap Remove Account.

5. Tap OK to confirm the removal of the account.

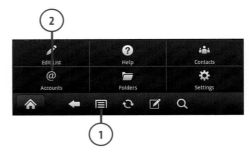

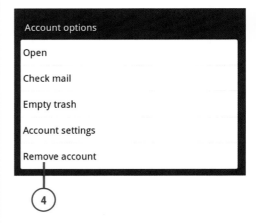

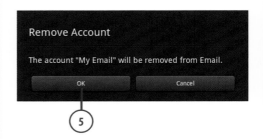

Managing Your Email Inbox

Your inbox is where you can view all of the email messages that have been received. Without opening a mail message, you can see who sent the mail, the subject of the email, and a brief snippet of the message. You can flag your mail, sort your mail, and delete messages you aren't interested in as well.

Choosing an Inbox

Your inbox can display email messages from a single account or in a unified account view that shows all messages from all accounts.

1. From your inbox, tap the current account name.

2. Select a different account to view the inbox for that account.

3. Select Unified Inbox to view the inbox for all accounts in a unified view.

Choosing a Folder

Most email providers allow you to create folders so that you can organize email that you want to keep. You can choose which folder is displayed when viewing an account's inbox.

It's Not All Good

Creating Folders

You can't create folders on your Kindle Fire. To create folders for your email account, you'll have to use an email program on your computer. Some email providers also provide a Web interface that you can use for creating folders and managing your email.

1. From your inbox, tap the Menu icon.

2. Tap Folders.

3. Select a folder to display that folder.

4. Tap to load messages from the selected folder.

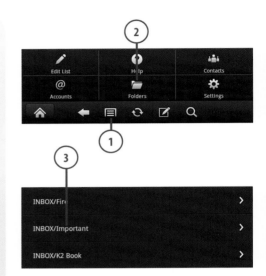

Loading Messages

Your inbox loads 25 messages at a time. You can tap to load another 25 messages.

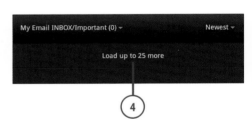

Sorting Email

By default, email is sorted with the newest emails listed first. You can change this sort order.

1. Tap the current sort order.

2. Tap the desired sort order to re-sort your inbox.

Searching Email

You can search your email messages. Only email messages that have been downloaded are searched. Search only displays results for the current folder.

1. Tap the Search icon.

2. Enter the text you want to search for. Your Kindle Fire can search the email address, subject, and message text.

3. Tap Search on the keyboard.

4. Tap a message from your search results in order to open the message for viewing.

Shortcut to Search

You can also access the search box by swiping down when you're at the top of your inbox.

Synchronizing Email

If you chose a poll frequency of Manual when you set up your account, your Kindle Fire only checks for mail when you manually synchronize mail. You can also manually synchronize mail at any time to check for new messages between polling intervals.

1. From one of your mailboxes, tap the Synchronize icon.

2. Tap Load Up To 25 More at the bottom of the list of messages in order to load additional messages if necessary. (The Kindle Fire only retrieves 25 messages at a time.)

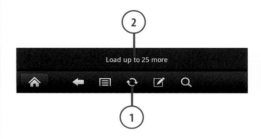

Selecting and Managing Multiple Messages

You can select one or more messages in your inbox. You can then choose to delete the messages, move them to another folder, or mark them as read or unread.

1. Swipe right on a message you want to select.

2. Tap other email messages to select them.

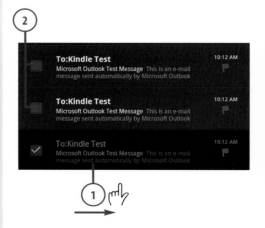

3. Tap the checkbox at the bottom of the screen to select all messages in the current folder.

4. Tap Mark as Read to mark all messages read.

5. Tap Mark as Unread to mark messages as unread. (Only available if all selected messages are currently marked as read.)

6. Tap Move to move the selected messages to another folder.

7. Choose a folder to move the messages.

8. Tap Delete to delete the selected messages.

9. Tap Done when finished or swipe left on any message.

Another Way of Selecting

You can also select multiple messages by tapping the Menu icon, tapping Edit List, and then checking the messages you want to select.

Accessing Email Settings

There are several configuration settings available for your account. They
are all available in the Settings
screen. All settings changes apply
only to the account you are viewing.
If you want a setting to apply to all
accounts, you must change the setting for each account.

To access the email Settings screen,
while viewing the inbox for your
account, tap the Menu icon and then
tap Settings.

Changing Polling Frequency

You can change the polling frequency that you selected during the initial
setup of your email account.

1. While in the Settings screen for
   the desired account, tap Fetch
   New Messages.

2. Select a new poll frequency.

IMAP Polling Frequency

IMAP accounts only list Manual
and Push for polling frequency.
Push downloads new messages
as they are available. Manual only
downloads messages when you
manually synchronize.

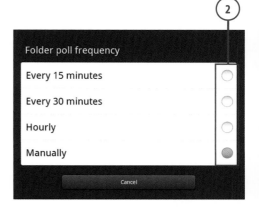

Controlling What Happens When Mail Is Deleted

By default, deleted messages are not deleted from your email server. (IMAP accounts other than Gmail are an exception. When you delete a message from a non-Gmail IMAP account, it is deleted from the server.) You can change the default behavior from the Settings screen for the account you want to modify.

1. Tap When I Delete a Message.

2. Tap to select what happens when a message is deleted.

3. Check Sync Server Deletions if you want mail deleted from another device or computer to also be deleted from your inbox on your Kindle Fire.

Adding a Notification Sound

By default, no sound is played when new email arrives. You can add a notification sound from the Settings screen for the account you want to modify.

1. Scroll to the bottom of the Settings screen.

2. Tap Notification Sound.

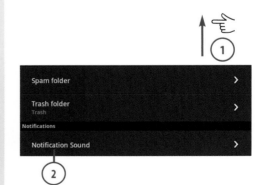

3. Select a notification sound. The sound plays when you tap the sound option.

4. Tap OK when you have chosen a sound that you like.

Emptying the Trash

After you've deleted messages, you can empty the trash to remove them from the folder that contains deleted items.

1. Tap the Menu icon.

2. Tap Folders.

3. Tap the Menu icon.

4. Tap Empty Trash.

Faster Trash Emptying

While you're on the Accounts screen, tap and hold an account and tap Empty Trash to empty the trash for that account.

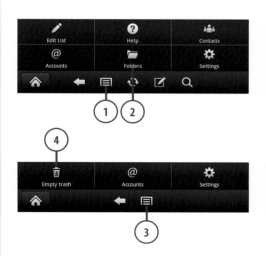

Flagging a Message

You can flag a message so that you can more easily locate it later.

1. From one of your email folders, tap the flag to mark a message as flagged.

2. If a message is already flagged, tap the flag to unflag it.

3. Sort by Flagged to easily locate flagged messages.

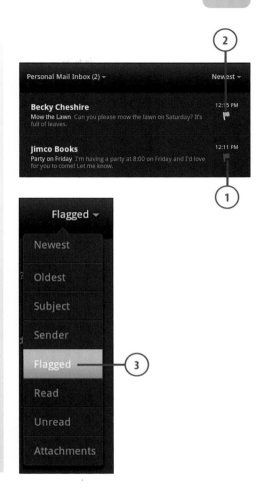

Reading Mail

Having email on your Kindle Fire is a great convenience. Not only is it nice to browse through your mail while you relax on the couch, but it's also easy to triage your email from the Kindle Fire. By that, I mean that you can quickly peruse your inbox and delete junk mail or other mail you're not interested in, move mail to another folder, mark important mail for follow-up later, and so forth.

Reading a Message

While reading a message, you can view information about the message, mark it as spam, move it to another folder, or delete the message.

1. Tap a message to open it.

2. Tap the header to display the address to which the mail was sent and the CC list.

3. Tap the flag to flag the message.

4. Tap Previous to view the previous message in your inbox.

5. Tap Next to view the next message in your inbox.

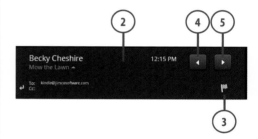

6. Tap the Trash icon to delete the message.

7. Tap the Menu icon and tap Move to move the message to another folder.

8. Tap the Menu icon and tap Mark as Spam to move the message to your junk mail folder.

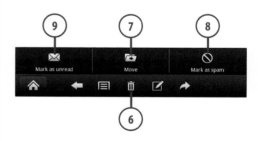

9. Tap the Menu icon and tap Mark as Unread to mark the message as unread.

10. To reply to or forward the message, tap the Reply icon.

11. Tap Reply to reply to the sender.

12. Tap Reply All to reply to the sender and other recipients.

13. Tap Forward to forward the message and any attachments to a new recipient.

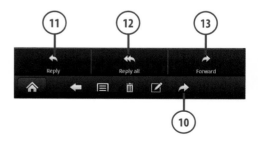

Choosing When Images Are Displayed

Some emails might contain images that are embedded within the email text. You can control when these images are displayed from the Settings screen.

1. From the Settings screen of the account you want to modify, tap Always Show Images.

2. Tap to select when images should be displayed.

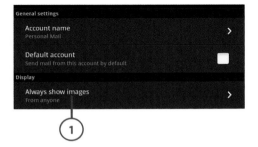

Why Not Display Images?

Images that are added inline to an email message are sometimes not actually part of the message. Instead, they may reside on another computer on the Internet. When these images are displayed, your Kindle Fire initiates a connection with the other computer in order to download the images. Because you don't control where that connection is going, it's a good idea to prevent the display of images unless the sender of the email is someone you know.

Another reason you might want to hide images is to prevent images from downloading to your Kindle Fire. If images aren't displayed, they won't be downloaded to your device where they will take up valuable storage space.

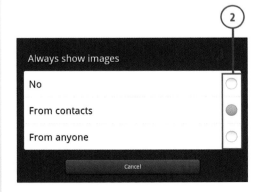

Viewing Attachments

Some email messages have one or more files attached that you can view. Your Kindle Fire comes with apps that can view many file types, including images, some videos, PDF files, and Microsoft Office documents.

1. Tap a mail message containing an attachment. (A paper clip is displayed on messages that contain an attachment.)

2. Tap Open to open the attachment.

3. Tap Save to save the attachment to your Kindle Fire. (Attachments are saved to the Download folder on your device.)

Opening Saved Attachments

You can use an app such as ES File Explorer to view the contents of your Download folder and open saved attachments. For details on using ES File Explorer, see the "Indispensable Apps" section in Chapter 8.

Sending Messages

You can send emails from your Kindle Fire. You can attach files to your emails so that you can share pictures or other files with others. You can also specify a signature that is added automatically to the emails that you send.

Composing a New Email Message

You can compose a new email message while viewing your inbox or while viewing an email message.

1. Tap the New Mail icon.

2. Enter an email address to which the message should be sent. Separate multiple emails with a comma.

3. Tap + to select a contact.

4. Tap a contact to add him or her to the recipient list. For more information on using contacts, see the "Working with Contacts" section later in this chapter.

5. Tap Cc\Bcc to display the Cc and Bcc fields.

6. Enter an email address to Cc if desired.

7. Enter an email address to Bcc if desired.

8. Enter a subject for your message.

9. Enter the text of the message.

10. Tap Attach to attach a file to your message.

11. Choose an app to use for browsing to the file you want to attach.

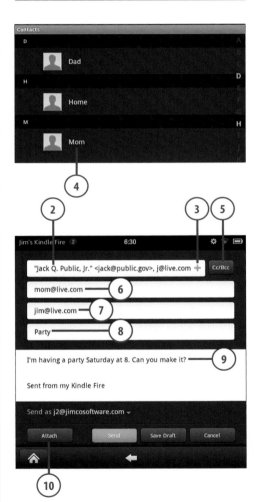

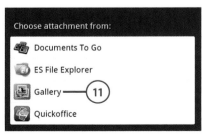

12. Select the file you want to attach using the app you selected.

13. Tap Send As to change the email address used to send the mail message.

14. Tap the X to remove a previously attached file.

15. Tap Save Draft to save a draft of your message that you can complete later. (Drafts are saved to the Drafts folder.)

16. Tap Send to send your message.

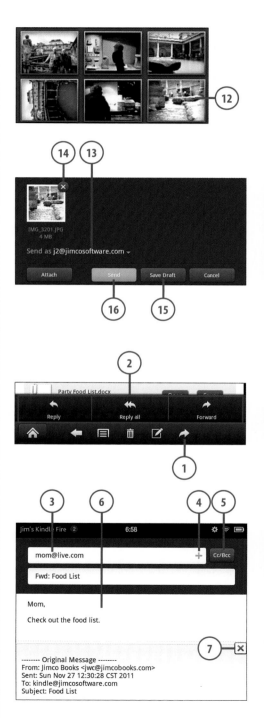

Sending Replies or Forwards

You can reply to or forward an email message that you have received.

1. While reading the email, tap the Reply icon.

2. Tap Reply, Reply All, or Forward.

3. Enter an email address if desired. (When replying, the sender's email address is added automatically.)

4. Tap + to add one of your contacts.

5. Tap Cc/Bcc to copy or blind copy a recipient.

6. Enter your message text.

7. Tap X to remove the original message if it's included.

8. Tap Quote Message to add the original message to your message if desired.

9. If a forwarded message contains an attachment, tap the X to remove the attachment if you prefer.

10. Tap Send As and select the email address from which the email should be sent.

11. Tap Attach to add an attachment.

12. Tap Save Draft to save a draft of the message.

13. Tap Send to send the message.

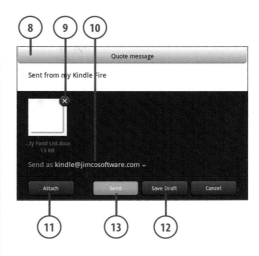

Creating a Signature

You can create a signature that is automatically added to all of your email messages. By default, the signature line reads "Sent from my Kindle Fire." You can change that to whatever text you choose, or you can remove the signature entirely. It's your choice.

1. From the Settings screen for the desired account, tap Composition Defaults.

2. Check the Use Signature box.

3. Enter your signature.

4. Choose where you would like the signature to appear.

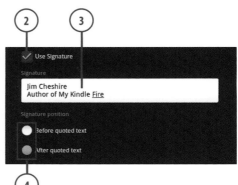

5. Tap the keyboard icon on the keyboard.

6. Tap Back to return to your inbox.

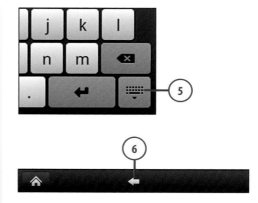

Sending Messages in Plain Text

By default, messages are created in HTML format so that the formatting and inline images of the original message are preserved. You can choose to send messages in plain text instead. Some people prefer plain text email over HTML email because hidden code can't be added to plain text email and it's more secure.

1. From the Settings screen for the desired account, tap Message Format.

2. Tap Plain Text.

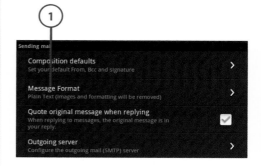

Changing Whether Original Message Is Quoted

By default, when you reply to or forward a message, the original message is quoted at the bottom of your message. You can turn off this feature if you don't like it. If you do turn off this feature, you can still add a quote of the original message to individual emails.

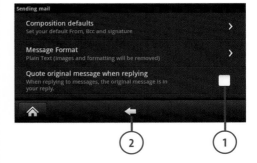

1. From the Settings screen for the desired account, tap Quote Original Message When Replying to clear the checkbox.

2. Tap Back to return to your inbox.

Working with Contacts

Your Kindle Fire's Contacts app makes it easy to maintain a list of contacts for email messages or for reference. You can easily import contacts from another source to your Kindle Fire. If you make changes to your contacts on the Kindle Fire and you want to apply those changes to your contact list in another email application, you can export your Kindle Fire contacts so that you can use them elsewhere.

Viewing Contacts

You can view your contacts from the Contacts app.

1. Open the Contacts app.

2. Tap All to view all of your contacts.

3. Tap Favorites to view your favorite contacts.

4. Tap a letter to jump to contacts that start with that letter.

5. Scroll to see more contacts.

6. Tap a contact to view contact details.

Favorite Contacts

You can add a contact to your favorites list by tapping and holding on the contact and then tapping Add to Favorites.

Adding a Contact

You can add a contact from the Contacts app.

1. Open the Contacts app.

2. Tap the Menu icon.

3. Tap New Contact.

Adding Pictures for Contacts

When I want to add a picture for a contact, I take a picture with my cell phone and email it to myself. I can then save the attachment on my Kindle Fire and add the picture to my contact.

4. Tap the picture icon to add a picture for the contact. (The picture must already be on your device.)

5. Enter the name information for your contact.

6. Tap Home and select a new type for the phone number if necessary.

7. Enter a phone number.

8. Tap + to add a new phone number for the contact.

9. Tap Home to change the type of email address if necessary.

10. Enter the email address.

11. Tap + if you want to add an additional email address.

12. Tap + if you want to add a mailing address.

13. Tap + if you want to add organization information.

14. Tap Save Changes.

Editing a Contact

You can edit an existing contact.

1. Tap and hold a contact in your contact list.

2. Tap Edit Contact.

3. Edit the information as necessary
    and tap Save Changes.

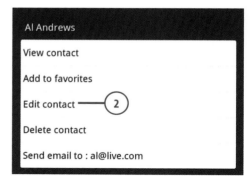

Changing Contact Sort Order and Name Display

You can change how your contact
names are displayed and the sort
order of your contacts.

1. From your contact list, tap the
    Menu icon.

2. Tap Settings.

3. Tap Sort List By to change sort order between first name and last name.

4. Tap View Contact Names As to switch from first name first to last name first.

Importing Contacts

It's likely that you already have a list of contacts either in the cloud or in another email application. You can import these contacts to your Kindle Fire.

Contacts must be in vCard format in order to be imported. If your email application can't export existing contacts in vCard format, there are numerous free utilities available that can convert common formats to vCard format.

Where are my vCards?

If you use an email application on your computer that stores contacts in vCard format, you should be able to locate them by searching your computer. Their location varies based on where the application stores information.

If you are converting existing contacts to vCard format, you specify where you want your vCards to be saved when you do the conversion. That's the location you'll want to use when importing your vCards into your Kindle Fire.

1. Connect your Kindle Fire to your computer and copy a folder containing your vCards to your Kindle Fire. It doesn't matter where you put them on your Kindle Fire, but I prefer to put mine in a Contacts folder so that I can identify them later.

2. Disconnect your Kindle Fire.

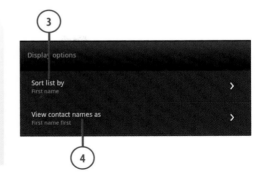

3. From your contact list, tap the Menu icon.

4. Tap Import/Export.

5. Tap Import from Internal Storage.

6. Select Import All vCard Files to import all vCards to your Kindle Fire.

7. Select Import One vCard File or Import Multiple vCard Files to choose which vCards to import.

8. Tap OK.

9. Tap the contacts that you would like to import.

10. Tap OK to import the selected contacts.

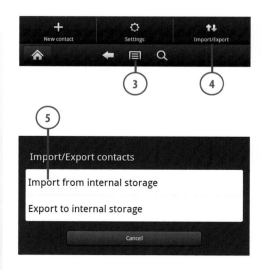

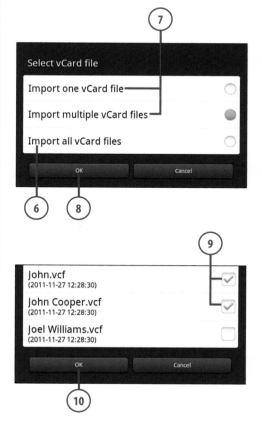

Exporting Contacts

You can export your contacts to a single vCard. If you export your contacts and save them somewhere other than on your Kindle Fire, you can import them to a new Kindle Fire device or after resetting your existing Kindle Fire.

1. From your contact list, tap the Menu icon.

2. Tap Import/Export.

3. Tap Export to Internal Storage.

4. Tap OK to confirm that you want to export your contacts. You'll see a message telling you the name of the vCard file that contains your exported contacts. You'll need to copy that file from your Kindle Fire to a computer.

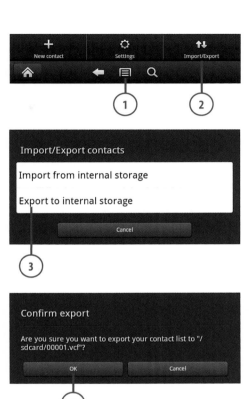

Make Note of the vCard Filename

Make note of the filename in the confirmation dialog when exporting contacts. That's the file that you should back up to someplace safe.

It's Not All Good

Disconnected Contacts

Contacts on your Kindle Fire are disconnected from the cloud. In other words, if you add a new contact on your Kindle Fire, that new contact will not automatically become available in the contact list you use for other devices. It would have been nice had Amazon included a contact app that accessed your online contacts from Gmail, Windows Live, or other email services. If you want that capability, you'll need to download an app from the Appstore. There are several available.

Use Tabs

Browse
Websites

Save and Access
Bookmarks

In this chapter, you'll learn how to use Silk, the web browser that's included with your Kindle Fire.

Browsing the Web with Silk

Your Kindle Fire includes a web browser called Silk. Silk is a full-featured browser with support for most of today's modern web standards. Silk also supports Adobe Flash and incorporates cloud technology to speed browsing.

You'll likely find that browsing on a tablet device is a mixed bag. Some sites will look and work great while others might not work as well. It can often be difficult to tap on a specific link when hyperlinks on a page appear too close to each other. (You can solve that problem by zooming on the page.) Even with these drawbacks, having the ability to browse the Internet easily from your favorite chair is a great convenience.

Browsing the Web

Silk works similarly to the web browser you use on your computer. One major difference is that instead of using a mouse, you use touch to navigate with Silk.

In this section, you'll learn the basics of using Silk. In the sections that follow, you'll learn about additional features such as using favorites and tabs.

Browsing to a Website

You can enter a URL and browse directly to a website.

1. From the Home screen, tap Web to launch Silk

2. Tap inside the address bar.

3. Enter a URL.

4. Tap Go.

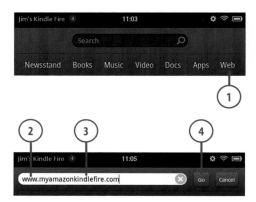

Navigating a Page

Web pages open full screen. You can navigate the page using zoom and pan techniques.

1. Browse to a URL.

2. Double-tap an area to zoom in.

3. Drag to move around the page.

4. Reverse pinch to zoom on the page.

5. Pinch to zoom out on the page.

6. Tap a link to follow the link.

7. Double-tap to zoom back to full page view.

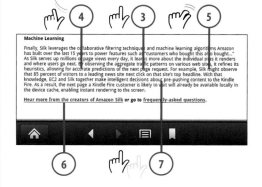

Sharing Pages on Facebook

When you find a page that you'd like to share with your Facebook friends, you can do it easily.

1. From the page that you want to share, tap the Menu icon.

2. Tap Share Page.

3. Tap Facebook.

4. Enter your Facebook login credentials if prompted and tap Log In.

5. Enter a comment.

6. Tap Post to Profile.

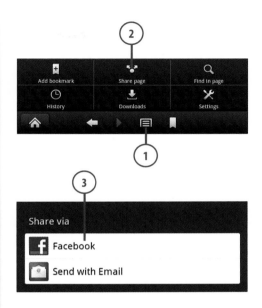

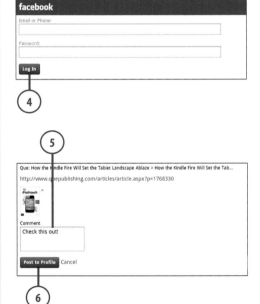

Sharing Pages with Email

You can also share a page by sending a link through email.

1. From the page that you want to share, tap the Menu icon.

2. Tap Share Page.

3. Tap Send with Email.

4. Enter one or more email addresses.

5. Add a message if desired.

6. Tap Send As and choose the email account you want to use when sending the email if you need to.

7. Tap Send.

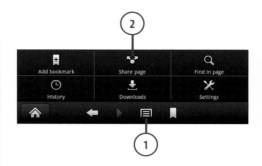

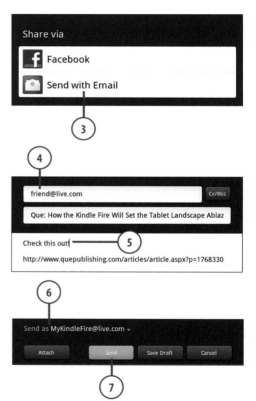

Copying a Link to the Current Page

You can copy a link to the current page so that you can paste it into a document.

1. Scroll to the top of the page so that the URL is visible.

2. Tap and hold the URL in the address bar.

3. Tap Copy to copy the URL so that you can paste it elsewhere.

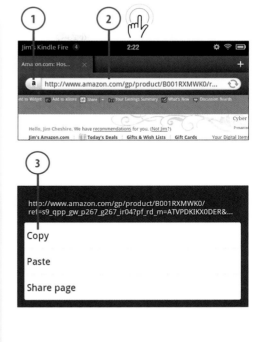

Copying a Hyperlink on a Page

You can also copy a hyperlink that appears on a page.

1. Tap and hold a hyperlink.

2. Tap Copy Link URL.

Saving Images

If you tap and hold on an image on a web page, you'll have the option to save the image.

Searching in the Current Page

You might want to search for text within the current page.

1. While viewing the page, tap the Menu icon.

2. Tap Find in Page.

3. Enter your search term. As you type, search results are highlighted.

4. Tap the Next Result icon to highlight the next result.

5. Tap the Previous Result icon to highlight the previous result.

6. Tap Done to stop searching.

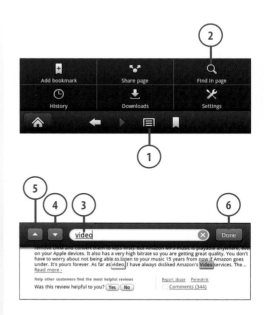

Searching the Web

You can easily search the Web from the address bar in Silk.

1. Scroll to the top of the page so that the address bar is visible.

2. Tap the address bar.

3. Enter your search term. The URL that was in the address bar is replaced with what you type.

4. Tap Go or tap a search suggestion to search using your configured search engine.

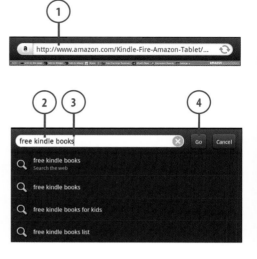

Your Search Engine

The default search engine is Google, but you can change it in Silk's settings. I show you how later in this chapter.

Working with Tabs

After you tap a link on a website, you can always tap the Back button to return to the previous page, but using tabs is much more convenient. Tabs allow you to have more than one web page open at the same time. You can flip between pages by tapping on the tab that contains the page you want to view.

Because each tab is using some resources on your Kindle Fire, Silk limits you to a total of up to 10 tabs.

Opening Links in a New Tab

When you click a link, the new page opens in the same tab by default. However, you can choose to open a link in a new tab so that you can have both the original page and the new page open at the same time.

1. Tap and hold a link that you want to follow.

2. Tap Open in New Tab.

3. Tap the original tab to return to the previous page.

Adding a New Tab and Closing Tabs

You can add a new tab so that you can browse to a new page while leaving the current page open in a different tab. You can then close a single tab or multiple tabs.

1. Tap the Add Tab icon to add a new tab.

2. Tap the Close icon to close a tab.

3. Tap and hold a tab to close multiple tabs.

4. Tap Close Other Tabs to close all tabs except for the active tab.

5. Tap Close All Tabs to close all tabs.

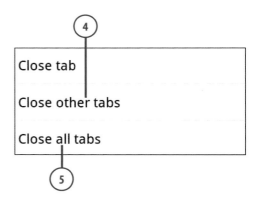

Always One Tab

Even if you tap Close All Tabs, one tab will remain open and will display your bookmarks as thumbnails. If you tap the Close icon on this tab, Silk closes and you are returned to your Kindle Fire's Home screen.

Navigating Many Tabs

If you open many tabs, there won't be enough room to display all of them at once. You have to scroll horizontally to see all of the tabs.

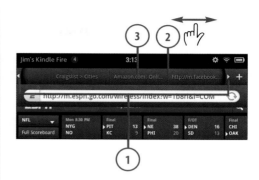

1. When Silk doesn't have enough room to display all tabs, arrows on the right and left of the screen indicate additional tabs.

2. Swipe to locate the desired tab.

3. Tap the tab to make it the active tab.

Using Bookmarks

Bookmarks are an easy way to return to a page at any time. Bookmarks aren't just convenient for saving your favorite sites. You can also use them to temporarily save links to websites while you are researching a particular topic. For example, when I'm trying to make a buying decision on a particular product, I'll often save bookmarks to reviews of the product so that I can easily refer back to them during my research.

Bookmarking the Current Page

You can bookmark any page that you are currently viewing.

1. While viewing the page, tap the Bookmark icon to see thumbnails of all of the pages you've already bookmarked.

2. Tap the page thumbnail that appears before the thumbnailed bookmarks to add a new bookmark for the current page.

3. Enter a name for your bookmark.

4. Edit the location (URL) if desired.

5. Tap OK to save the bookmark.

Bookmarking a Hyperlink

You can also bookmark a hyperlink without following the hyperlink.

1. Tap and hold the hyperlink that you want to bookmark.

2. Tap Bookmark Link.

3. Enter a name for your bookmark.

4. Edit the location (URL) if desired.

5. Tap OK to save your bookmark.

Viewing and Following Bookmarks

You can view your bookmarks in one place and follow a bookmark easily.

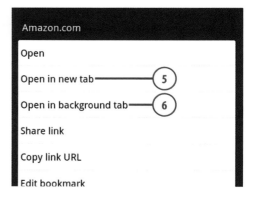

1. Tap the Bookmark icon to open the Bookmarks screen.

2. Tap the List View icon to view your bookmarks in a list.

3. Tap the Grid View icon to view your bookmarks in a grid, like the view shown here.

4. Tap a bookmark to go the book-marked page.

5. To open a bookmark in a new tab, tap and hold the bookmark and tap Open in New Tab.

6. To open a bookmark in a new tab but without making the new tab the active tab, tap and hold the bookmark and tap Open in Background Tab.

Editing a Bookmark

You can edit the name or the location of a bookmark.

1. From the Bookmarks screen, tap and hold the bookmark you want to edit.

2. Tap Edit Bookmark.

3. Make the desired changes to your bookmark.

4. Tap OK to save the bookmark.

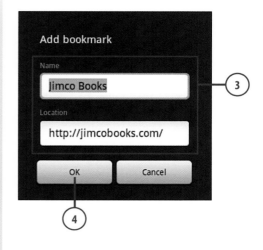

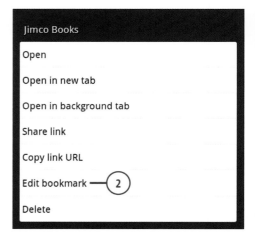

Deleting a Bookmark

You can delete a bookmark from the Bookmarks screen.

1. Tap and hold the bookmark you want to delete.

2. Tap Delete.

3. Tap OK to delete the bookmark.

Using History

As you browse the Web, Silk keeps a record of where you've been in the browser history. Silk stores your history for the past seven days of browsing.

Viewing History

You can view your browsing history so that you can easily return to a page you've previously visited.

1. While browsing, tap the Menu icon.

2. Tap History.

3. Tap a section to expand and collapse history by date.

4. Tap an item in history to return to that page.

5. Tap an empty bookmark icon to add a bookmark for the item.

6. Tap a filled bookmark icon to remove a bookmark for the item.

7. Tap Clear All to clear history.

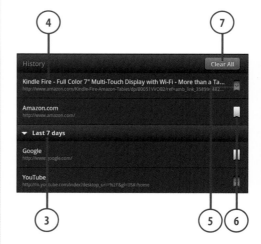

Searching History

To locate a history item more easily, you can search for a specific term. When searching your history, only the URL and the history item's name is searched. Content on the page linked to by the history item is not searched.

1. While viewing history, tap the Search icon.

2. Tap in the search box.

3. Enter your search term. Search results appear as you type.

4. History items show a clock icon. Tap a history item to go to that page.

5. Tap the search icon labeled Search the Web to do a Web search for your search term.

Deleting a Single History Item

If you'd prefer to delete one or more history items instead of clearing all history items, you can do so from the History screen.

1. Tap and hold the history item you want to delete.

2. Tap Delete.

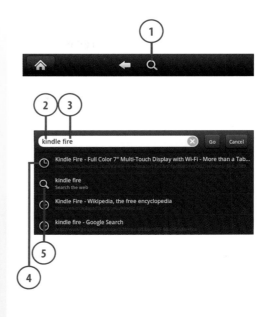

Downloading Files

You can download files using Silk. Files that are downloaded are available on the Downloads screen. You can access the Downloads screen by tapping the Menu icon while browsing and then tapping Downloads.

While it doesn't make sense to download some types of files (executable files that install software on a computer, for example), you might want to download eBook files, PDF files, pictures, or MP4 videos.

It's Not All Good

Be Cautious of Downloading Files

The Internet isn't always a safe place. Before you download a file, make sure you trust the source of the file. There are numerous Android viruses that can infect your Kindle Fire, and a common source of Android viruses is infected apps and files. You can keep yourself safe by only downloading files from known reputable websites. For example, if you're downloading a PDF manual of your new TV set from the manufacturer's website, you'll be fine. If you locate what appears to be a PDF manual from a different site, you'd be better off getting it from the manufacturer's site instead.

When you open a downloaded file, your Kindle Fire uses the file's extension (the letters after the period in the file's name) to determine what app you have that can handle opening the file. If you have more than one app installed that can open the file, you'll be prompted to select an app to use. You can also choose an app as the default app for that particular file type.

Starting and Monitoring Downloads

After starting a download, you can see a list of your downloads and monitor it easily.

1. Tap a downloadable link to start the download.

2. To monitor your download, tap the Menu icon.

3. Tap Downloads.

4. Tap a section to expand or collapse downloads by date.

5. Downloads that are active show as In Progress.

6. Downloads that have finished show as Complete.

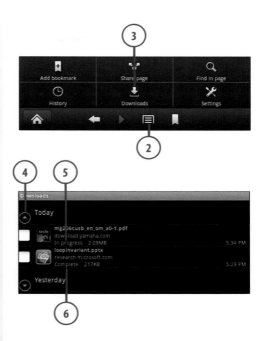

Canceling a Download

You can cancel a download before it completes.

1. Tap and hold a download that is in progress.

2. Tap Cancel to cancel the download.

Opening Downloaded Files

After a file has been downloaded, you can open it from the Downloads screen.

1. Tap a download that has completed.

2. Choose the application that you'd like to use to open the file if prompted.

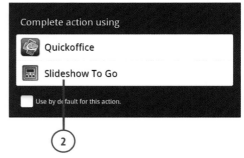

Deleting Downloaded Files

You can delete downloaded files to free up space on your Kindle Fire.

1. From the Downloads screen, tap the checkbox to check the downloads you want to delete.

2. Tap Delete to delete the selected downloads.

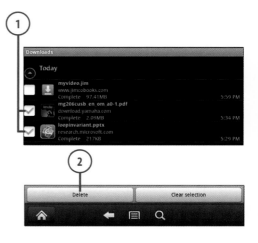

Configuring Silk Settings

There are several settings in Silk that help you to get the most out of your Kindle Fire. I don't cover all of the settings here, but I do cover the ones that are the most useful.

All of Silk's settings are on the Settings screen. To access the Settings screen, tap the Menu icon while browsing and then tap the Settings icon. Here's an initial look at the groups of settings you'll find.

Behavior Settings

Advanced Settings

Swipe down on the Settings screen to see more settings.

Setting Your Search Engine

You can choose which search engine is used when you search the Web.

1. Tap Set Search Engine.

2. Choose a search engine.

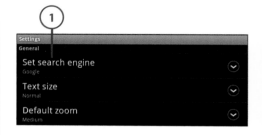

Changing Text Size

If you find the text size in Silk to be too small or too large, you can adjust it to your liking.

1. Tap Text Size.

2. Choose a text size.

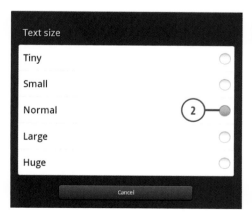

Controlling Cookies

Cookies are small files saved to your browser when a website needs to store information specific to you that it can use on your subsequent visits to the site. For example, many websites allow you to log in using a username and password so that they can offer you a more personalized experience. When you log in, the site may save your authentication information in a cookie that it can use to automatically log you in when you come back to the site. If you want to clear information that a site is storing for you, you can delete cookies. You might want to do this if a site is behaving strangely or if you just want to remove all information a site is saving on your Kindle Fire.

1. Tap to clear the Accept Cookies checkbox if you don't want Silk to use cookies.

2. Tap Clear All Cookie Data to clear any cookies that Silk has stored.

3. Tap OK to clear the cookies.

Clearing the Cache

Silk caches (stores) pages as you browse so that they load faster on subsequent visits. Over time this can accumulate a lot of data you might not need. You can clear this cache to free up some extra space.

1. Tap Clear Cache.
2. Tap OK to confirm.

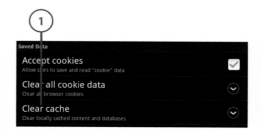

Clearing History

In addition to clearing your browser's history from within the Silk browser, you can also clear it from the Settings page.

1. Tap Clear History.
2. Tap OK to confirm.

Controlling Form and Password Data

By default, Silk saves data you enter into forms and prompts you to save passwords. You can disable these features and clear saved data.

1. Tap to clear the Remember Form Data check if you don't want Silk to remember form data.

2. To clear form data, tap Clear Form Data.

3. Tap OK to confirm.

4. Tap to clear the check on Remember Passwords if you don't want Silk to prompt you to remember passwords.

5. Tap Clear Passwords to delete any saved passwords.

6. Tap OK to confirm.

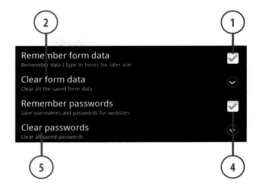

Accelerating Page Loading

By default, Silk attempts to accelerate page loading by funneling all of your browsing traffic through Amazon's servers and attempting to serve you a cloud version of a page stored on Amazon's servers when applicable. This is supposed to speed up browsing, but tests have shown that it doesn't seem to help much. If you'd like, you can turn this feature off.

1. Tap to clear the check on Accelerate Page Loading to turn off the feature.

2. Tap to check the box to re-enable the feature.

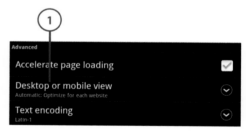

Setting Your Silk View

When you visit a website, the website detects what browser you're using. When you visit a site using a mobile device or a tablet, some sites serve you a site with a minimalistic, mobile-friendly design. You can use the Desktop or Mobile View setting to control whether this happens.

1. Tap Desktop or Mobile View.

2. Select Desktop to always view sites using the non-mobile version.

3. Select Mobile to always show an optimized view for mobile devices if available.

4. Select Automatic (the default setting) to let the website determine how to display the page.

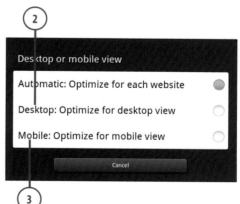

>> Go Further

IDENTIFYING YOUR BROWSER

When you visit a website, your web browser sends information that allows the website to determine what kind of device you're using to access the site. Websites can use this information to decide how to display the site in a way that works best with your device.

When you visit a website using Silk on your Kindle Fire, the website sees the following information.

```
Mozilla/5.0 (Macintosh; U; Intel Mac OS X 10_6_3; en-us;
Silk/1.1.0-84) AppleWebKit/533.16 (KHTML, like Gecko)
Version/5.0 Safari/533.16 Silk-Accelerated=true
```

This information (called a *user-agent string*) tells the website that you're using Silk version 1.1.0-84. The website developer can use this information to serve you the site formatted in a way that looks best on the Kindle Fire.

Incidentally, you may also notice that Silk identifies itself as running on a Macintosh running OS X. It's pretty common for user-agent strings to lie about what kind of device they are coming from, but it is a bit strange to see the Kindle Fire reporting that it's running on a Mac. Stranger still, the user-agent string on the initial builds of the Kindle Fire showed it was running on Linux, a completely different operating system. In fact, the Kindle Fire (as you know by now) runs on Android. Go figure.

Index

C

W

X-Y-Z

MAKE THE MOST OF YOUR SMARTPHONE, TABLET, COMPUTER, AND MORE!
CHECK OUT THE MY...BOOK SERIES

ISBN 13: 9780789748256

ISBN 13: 9780789748928

ISBN 13: 9780789748942

ISBN 13: 9780789749383

Full-Color, Step-by-Step Guides

The "My..." series is a visually rich, task-based series to help you get up and running with your new device and technology, and tap into some of the hidden, or less obvious, features. The organized, task-based format allows you to quickly and easily find exactly the task you want to accomplish, and then shows you how to achieve it with minimal text and plenty of visual cues.

**Visit quepublishing.com/mybooks to learn more
about the My... book series from Que.**

quepublishing.com

FREE Online Edition

Your purchase of **My Kindle Fire** includes access to a free online edition for 45 days through the Safari Books Online subscription service. Nearly every Que book is available online through Safari Books Online, along with more than 5,000 other technical books and videos from publishers such as Addison-Wesley Professional, Cisco Press, Exam Cram, IBM Press, O'Reilly, Prentice Hall, and Sams.

SAFARI BOOKS ONLINE allows you to search for a specific answer, cut and paste code, download chapters, and stay current with emerging technologies.

Activate your FREE Online Edition at www.informit.com/safarifree

> **STEP 1:** Enter the coupon code: RUDYDDB.

> **STEP 2:** New Safari users, complete the brief registration form.
> Safari subscribers, just log in.

If you have difficulty registering on Safari or accessing the online edition, please e-mail customer-service@safaribooksonline.com